W9-BUX-197

The Great Fire
of London

The Great Fire of London

DAVID A. WEISS

Drawings by Joseph Papin

CUMBERLAND ENTERPRISES, INC.

New York

WINGATE COLLEGE LIBRARY

To My Father

© 1968, 1992 by David A. Weiss

All rights reserved. No part of this book may be reproduced, stored
in a retrieval system, or transmitted, in any form or by any means,
electronic, mechanical, photocopying, recording, or otherwise, without
written permission of the publisher.

Library of Congress Catalog Number: 68-9058

Printed in the United States of America

COVER DESIGN: BERNARD SCHLEIFER

Printed by: Daamen, Inc.

Table of Contents

NOTE TO THE READER

The City of London—identified as the City—as distinguished from the city of London—Greater London—extended for a mile along the Thames, from Fleet Ditch to the Tower, a square-mile area that at the time of the Great Fire held an estimated 600,000 inhabitants.

I

Saturday and Sunday, September 1 and 2, 1666

A great fire in the city . . .

IN RESTORATION ENGLAND, the busiest day of the week was Saturday, and September 1, 1666, in London was no exception. Since early morning, carts, carriages, and pedestrians, coming up from Southwark on the southern bank of the Thames River, had jammed London Bridge. They were trying to push across the Bridge's narrow, wooden roadway, lined on both sides by old, six-story Tudor houses which projected over the edges. If not for wooden supports, the houses would have fallen into the swirling waters below.

As their vehicles rattled over the Bridge, the occupants could catch a glimpse of London and the river—through gaps created several decades before, when some Bridge houses had burned down and were never rebuilt. The Thames was dotted with shipping. Merchantmen just in from the Indies tugged at anchor in midstream. Men-of-war alongside docks and warehouses were taking on naval stores. And hundreds of small boats and lighters moved up and down the river, rowed by sweaty watermen who carried passengers to and from boat stairs on the riverbank.

Three miles up the river, around a bend, was the city of Westminster where were located not only the famous Abbey, but also the many royal apartments and government buildings that made up Whitehall Palace, seat of the gov-

ernment of Charles II. Down a quarter-mile from Westminster was the Strand, where the wealthy and nobility
lived in spacious mansions with their own private boat
stairs and gardens running down to the river. Farther down
was the Temple, where London's lawyers studied and
worked. Then came Fleet Ditch, a small river whose pol-
luted water ran into the Thames.

Near Fleet Ditch was the beginning of the ancient
thirty-five-foot wall which enclosed the square mile that
was the City of London as distinguished from Greater
London. The City extended only a mile along the Thames,
from Fleet Ditch to the Tower of London, the ancient Norman fortress where the Mint was located and the Crown
Jewels kept. But packed into that small area were an estimated 600,000 inhabitants—one-tenth the population of all
England.

Once the carriages and carts crossed London Bridge,
they clattered over cobblestone streets. Narrow and
crooked, with rivers of garbage running down their cen-
ters, the streets ran every which way, and were connected
by a maze of alleys, courts, and lanes. Pedestrians always
had difficulty, for there were no sidewalks. Horse-drawn
coaches careening by splashed mud on walkers, who also
had to duck slops tossed out of second-story windows.
When it rained, rainwater bounced off roofs into their
faces. Rain or shine, they coughed and sputtered from the
clouds of irritating black smoke that continually hung over
London—the product of breweries, soap boilers, and tanneries within the City walls.

London's Tudor houses, which were built mostly of
timber and lath and plaster, faced the streets with uneven
frontages. To prevent carriages from running into them,

LONDON BEFORE THE FIRE

each house had a post in front which acted as a bumper. The second stories of most houses protruded over the street, often blocking out the light. Many houses doubled as shops, with painted signs over their doors, and apprentices standing in doorways, calling out, "What d'ye lack, ladies?"

Milkmaids pushed through the streets, selling milk in pails. Custardmongers hawked apples, and coalmen carried cobbles from Newcastle. In elegant carriages, preceded by footmen in bright livery, ladies of fashion rolled by on their way to shop for lace at Cheapside or for foreign cloths at the bazaar in Cornhill. Housewives crowded the markets at Leadenhall and the Stocks Market, buying fish, meat, and herbs.

At the Royal Exchange on that September Saturday in 1666, London's merchant-bankers talked excitedly about the new tobacco cargo just arrived from the colony of Virginia. Throughout the City, in the various Company Halls like Paynter-Stainers and Stationers, members of City Companies—the craft guilds of London—discussed such problems as lengthening the periods that apprentices should serve. At Guildhall, the ancient municipal building, London's aldermen and other members of the City's Common Council struggled with the metropolis' mounting problems. The City, no longer able to contain the increasing population, was losing inhabitants to the suburbs. Houses were being built and communities formed in the once grassy meadows and open fields outside the walls. Some of these parishes—particularly those in the Liberties, the nearest suburbs—were now part of Greater London, but what of the parishes farther away?

London's churches were also busy that Saturday, preparing for services on the morrow. The City had more than one hundred parish churches, their spires rising high over the jumbled houses. But dominating London's skyline was the massive structure of the mother church which sat high on Ludgate Hill near the wall in the west—St. Paul's, old and dilapidated, but still the largest cathedral in the Western world and the most impressive building in England.

By afternoon, the bustle began to abate. Thousands of Londoners returned home or repaired to one of the city's many taverns, where they downed tankards of ale. Those who lived outside London also went home, either back over London Bridge, or in a boat rowed by watermen, or through one of the seven ancient gates in the City's wall. The gates themselves Ludgate, Aldersgate, Newgate, and the others were so large that most contained compters or prisons.

By late afternoon, most Londoners had eaten supper— the nobles, attended by dozens of servants, dining on roast mutton; the poor huddled, sometimes twenty to a room, in tenements, eating stale bread and roots. By evening, except for those still on the streets or attending a play at the theatre on Drury Lane, the City was still except for the creaking of signs on iron hinges as an east wind began to blow over London. The few late carousers wending their way home, assisted by linkboys with lanterns, paid little attention to the wind. Neither did the constables nor the watch making the rounds, except to call out, "One before the clock and a strong wind."

On Pudding Lane, a narrow street near the approach to the London Bridge, Thomas Farynor, the King's Baker, was fast asleep. At ten o'clock he had drawn his ovens and gone to bed. But four hours later he was suddenly awakened by a servant screaming, "Fire! Fire!"

Jumping out of bed, Farynor took one look at the

smoke billowing up the stairs, and roused his family. With the servant, they escaped through an attic window to the roof of the house next door—all except a maidservant who, too frightened to climb over the roof, remained, and became in a few minutes the first casualty of the Great Fire of London.

As the Farynors got down to street level, neighbors gathered to watch the flames, and a few ran into a nearby church to fetch the leathern buckets of water which were stored in most public buildings for just such emergencies. But the water tossed on the flames was of no avail now that the wind was blowing so briskly.

Soon the gilded coach of Sir Thomas Bludworth, London's Lord Mayor, clattered up. Annoyed at having his sleep interrupted, Bludworth saw nothing unusual in the fire. Although almost every one of London's fifteen thousand houses was of wooden construction, the city had never had a serious fire. A hundred minor fires a year, yes, but seldom did any more than a dozen houses burn down.

When some of Farynor's neighbors asked if they should get fire hooks and pull down the houses adjoining, Bludworth shook his head. The time to pull down was when the fire seemed in danger of getting out of control. Only then did you get the long poles with hooks, attach the hooks to the house's ridge beams, and pull with teams of horses or men. Then the burning timbers were brought to the ground where they could be more easily beaten out; and a gap was left in the path of the fire.

No, this fire did not call for pulling down, Bludworth said as he stepped in his coach and returned home to bed.

But hardly had he left than the house next to Farynor's caught fire. Then sparks—gusted by the wind—landed in the yard of a nearby inn where hay had been stored. Soon houses all around were blazing.

Less than a quarter-mile away to the east, not far from the Tower of London, was Seething Lane, site of His Majesty's Navy Office. Also on Seething Lane, in homes provided by the Navy, lived several high-ranking Navy administrative officers, including Samuel Pepys, who as Clerk of the Acts served as secretary to the Navy Board.

Pepys and his wife Elizabeth were fast asleep, but their maid Jane, who had worked late with the other maids preparing Sunday's dinner, was awakened about 3 A.M. by a shutter banging from the wind. When Jane went to the window to fasten it, she noticed flames and smoke in the distance. Frightened, she ran into her master's bedroom.

"There's a great fire in the City," Jane said.

A fire! Wrapping a night-robe around his stocky frame, Pepys rushed into Jane's room. Yes, through the window, there it was! Orange flames shooting skyward! But like the Lord Mayor, Pepys did not see any cause for alarm unless the fire were almost next door. He reassured Jane and went back to bed.

Samuel Pepys had more pressing matters to think about. As secretary to the Navy Board, he had the important responsibility of keeping the Navy in supplies. The

English had been at war since 1664 with Holland. The
second Dutch war in a decade, it had the same origin as the
previous one: commercial rivalry over trade in the North
Sea and the East Indies. The English had precipitated the
present conflict by capturing the Dutch city of New Amsterdam in the New World, and by attacking a Dutch fort
in Africa. England declared war officially after Parliament
voted a war chest of two and one-half million pounds. The
Navy then outfitted its fleets, and in 1665 the English won
a tremendous naval victory off Lowestoft, putting a quarter
of the Dutch fleet out of action. Later, the Earl of Sandwich, Pepys's cousin, won another important naval engage-
ment. But this year, action had been inconclusive. All the
past summer the English fleets had been at sea, unsuccessfully trying to catch the Dutch Admiral De Ruyter.

At seven Sunday morning when Pepys rose again, he
remembered the fire and decided to give it a second look.
If anything, he thought to himself, the flames seemed farther away. But, as he was straightening his room, the maid
Jane entered.

"The fire we saw," she said. "It burned down three
hundred houses in the night."

Pepys reached for his curled wig. "Three hundred
houses" was the biggest fire he had ever heard of. He
wanted to see the flames better, and he knew an excellent
viewing spot—the Tower of London.

Donning his beaver hat, Pepys said a quick good-bye
to his wife, and headed toward the Tower. With the small
son of Sir John Robinson, Lieutenant of the Tower, Pepys
climbed up the stone steps of Bell Tower; with the wind
whistling around their ears, they looked out over the city.

The entire area around London Bridge was ablaze.

All the houses leading up to the Bridge were burning, and flames were approaching the docks and warehouses fronting the river. London Bridge itself was burning at both ends, and as Pepys watched with horrified eyes, one of the blazing houses on the Bridge collapsed and fell with burning timbers into the water.

After talking briefly to Sir John Robinson about the fire, Pepys walked to the boat stairs at the Tower of London and engaged a waterman to row him near the flames. As the waterman pushed the boat off with an oar, Pepys felt the spray blow in his face. It was the strong wind, he realized, that made this fire so dangerous. Also, during the summer before, London had experienced its worst dry spell in many years.

Pepys's spirits rose momentarily as the boat neared London Bridge. Up close he could see that the flames had been stopped on the end of the Bridge nearest Southwark, and that, on the London end, they had gotten only a third of the way down the Bridge, stopped by the gap of burned-down and un-rebuilt houses.

But farther up the river, beyond the Bridge, the story was different—the roaring flames and black smoke told Pepys that. He directed the waterman to go under the Bridge upstream. Nosing the boat in front of one of the Bridge's stone arches, the man pushed it through, and as they emerged with a splash, Pepys saw a "lamentable" sight. The entire riverfront for about a half mile was burning furiously. Several docks were ablaze, and as Pepys watched, a warehouse exploded suddenly, sending flames sky high.

For more than an hour, Pepys stayed in the boat, unable to turn his eyes away. Now houses farther back from the river were burning, and Pepys noticed that their occupants (for some strange reason) stayed in them until the last minute. Seemingly, only when the flames were a few feet away did these people start to flee. Then, in a frenzy, lugging their possessions and household goods, they would rush to the nearest boat stairs, desperately trying to rent boats to take them to safety either down the river or across to Southwark. Some who could find no boats hurled their possessions right into the Thames.

Pepys noticed that even the pigeons showed this same reluctance to leave their homes. Hovering around windows

Pepys sees fire from under arch of bridge

and balconies, some stayed too long—until flames reached their wings, sending them plummeting to earth.

To Pepys's amazement, no one seemed to be fighting the flames. Although London had no official fire-fighting force, its elected and appointed officials—the aldermen and constables—could have organized some kind of effort, he felt. Also, more homeowners and citizens could have tried to quench the flames with the water from the leathern buckets installed in the churches and public buildings.

Certainly, by this time, Pepys reasoned, no one still thought the fire was an ordinary one. While he was sitting in the boat, the fire not only spread northward into the City, but also advanced westward until it had almost reached the Steelyard, where the merchants of the Hanseatic League had their London headquarters.

Back from the river, Pepys could see St. Laurence Pountney, the church where his schoolmate Elborough was minister. No houses were burning at all near the church, but suddenly its tall steeple burst into flames, almost as if fired from within. Minutes later, melted lead ran down the steeple, and soon its timbers gave way. With a crash, the steeple collapsed, and Pepys in the boat felt sure he heard the falling bells of St. Laurence Pountney give one last horrible clang.

The fire was obviously out of control, and Pepys decided he should inform the Royal Court. Tapping the waterman on the shoulder, he pointed upstream to the bend in the river.

"Take me to Whitehall Palace," he directed.

At Whitehall, hundreds of the King's loyal subjects thronged the corridor of the Stone Gallery, waiting to see Charles II. Suddenly the velvet curtains to the royal apartments parted. Charles stepped out, followed by his brother, the Duke of York, and his ministers of state. Extremely tall, the King, who was somberly dressed, paused briefly as his subjects fell to their knees. He turned to them his swarthy face, topped by the large brown curled wig he wore to hide his graying hair, and then, after nodding and saying "God bless you" to three or four subjects he recognized, walked rapidly down the corridor toward the royal chapel.

Here, every Sunday before the eyes of visiting subjects, Charles prayed in public, just as he dined each day in public in the great banqueting hall. But no sooner did Charles reach the chapel, with his ministers and the Duke of York still at his heels, than a groom dressed in a richly embroidered coat entered and whispered in the ear of one of the ministers.

"It's Pepys of the Navy Office, your Majesty," the minister said. "He's outside with news about a fire in London out of control."

PEPYS REPORTS TO
KING CHARLES

Charles motioned to send Pepys in. That morning, when he had risen at dawn to play tennis in St. James's Park, he had seen flames from the palace windows. But he never thought . . .

Hat in hand, Pepys entered, bowing nervously. "Your Majesty," he started, his voice pitched high, and then he began describing the fire, how the wind was driving the flames westward along the Thames and north into the city.

Charles shook his head. A fire out of control in England's capital seemed like the last straw. Not only was the nation at war with the Dutch, but the year before, England had suffered the worst plague in its history, one from which it had still not fully recovered. An estimated seventy thousand Londoners had died, with as many as one thousand casualties a day. A man hale and hearty in the morning would be a corpse by nightfall, ready to be hauled away to the burial pits. Every pesthouse had been overcrowded, and every street in London had a red cross daubed on at least one door. Thousands had fled London, and Charles himself finally had to move the government and the Court away from the contagion.

Charles's entire life had been one of battling adversity. A boy when England's Civil War broke out, he was forced to flee after the Royalists' defeat. His father, Charles I, was executed; and Charles himself spent years of penniless exile in Holland and France before being restored triumphantly to his throne in 1660, after Cromwell died.

As king, his tasks were monumental. He had to heal the split between Royalists and Parliamentarians. He had to restore a sound financial basis to a nation bankrupted by debts. He had to revive commerce, try to mend the religious dissension between Protestant and Catholic, maneuver England through the pitfalls of European diplomacy, and lead her in a war—successful so far—against the powerful Dutch.

Yet, Charles had been criticized on all sides for evading his responsibilities. His detractors objected to his love of sport, his riding his own horses at the Newmarket races, taking long walks through St. James's Park in the morning, hunting stag in the forests near London, and sailing up the Thames in his private yacht. They said he wasted too much time in his laboratory on foolish scientific experiments. They resented the fact that he had married a Catholic—Catherine Braganza of Portugal. They complained about the money he spent on his many mistresses, especially the blonde courtesan Barbara Villiers, the Countess of Castlemaine, whom he had recently created the Duchess of Cleveland.

"Your Majesty," Pepys said, "I think that unless you command the houses to be pulled down, nothing will save the City."

Charles had come to the same conclusion himself. For centuries, ever since the time of London's first Lord Mayor, laws had been enacted in London barring new construction in any material except brick and stone. Queen Elizabeth I had sponsored such a law, and so had Charles. But no one had ever been able to enforce them—and now London was paying the penalty for this neglect.

Charles turned to his ministers. Pepys was right. The leathern buckets were of little value. Neither were the brass "squirts" that some City Companies had on hand, nor the "engines" or cisterns on wheels that a few Companies had recently purchased. Most of them could not get through London's narrow streets.

"Send word at once to collect all the fire hooks in Westminster and take them to London," Charles ordered his ministers. "Also set up a system of couriers to keep me informed hourly of the fire's advance."

Then Charles II turned to Pepys. "Ride into the City as fast as you can," he said. "Find the Lord Mayor, and tell him to spare no houses, but to pull down in every direction."

Pepys had never been so excited. Six years before, as private secretary to his cousin the Earl of Sandwich, he had been aboard the *Royal Charles,* the ship in which Sandwich had escorted Charles back from Holland to England and his restored throne. But even that mission was not as important as this. Quickly borrowing a coach, Pepys gave orders to the driver. "Make haste to St. Paul's. Royal business."

Pepys was soon bouncing over the cobblestones of Fleet Street leading to the City wall. A half hour later, when he reached London, the flames driven by the wind were advancing rapidly. The entire city was now alerted to the fire, and the churches—where earlier that morning regular services had been held—were now pealing their bells backwards, the traditional fire signal.

In those areas near the flames, Londoners were running from street to street, shouting, "Fire! Fire!" Hundreds were fleeing, and, ironically, hundreds of others were coming into the City to get a look at the destruction. William Taswell, a young student at Westminster School, first heard of the fire during the morning services in Westminster Abbey. Afterward, as he noticed people running to and fro and talking about the flames, he saw live sparks in the air that the wind had carried all the way from London.

PEOPLE FLEEING THE FIRE

Then, at the boat stairs, Taswell came across four Londoners disembarking from a lighter. They had escaped the flames, but had been able to carry away little more than some blankets they had around their shoulders. Taswell found a waterman with a boat to hire, and was soon on his way to London to see the fire.

When Pepys's carriage reached St. Paul's, he found the air heavy with smoke. In the distance, he heard flames crackling and women screaming. Walking eastward, he passed dozens of families coming toward him, loaded down with furniture and goods they were carrying to safety inside St. Paul's great courtyard. Carts, piled high with household possessions, were trying to get through the streets. But progress was slow, and as drivers cursed and shoved, one cart overturned, spilling its contents into the gutter of filth running down the center of the cobblestoned street.

On Cannon Street, Pepys found Sir Thomas Bludworth, the Lord Mayor, racing frantically around, a handkerchief around his neck. When Pepys delivered the King's orders, Bludworth cried out: "Lord, what can I do? I am spent. People will not obey me. I have been pulling down houses, but the fire overtakes us before we can do it."

Bludworth told Pepys that soldiers were not needed because the Trained Bands, the militia, had been called up. What he really needed, he said, was rest, since he had been up most of the night.

Walking back to his house in Seething Lane, Pepys noticed that everyone he passed seemed to be in a daze. Yet, as he had observed before, no one seemed to be doing anything to quench the flames. Smoke from the riverfront was getting blacker now, and Pepys guessed that more warehouses must be afire, since he could smell burning pitch and tar.

Home shortly after noon, Pepys found his wife Elizabeth waiting with their dinner guests. No one could talk of anything but the fire, and Pepys proudly told of his meeting with the King. The guests had other recent news. The Thames water system was out of commission. The big water wheels that pumped up water from the river and distributed it in wooden pipes throughout the central part of the City had been damaged when flames hit London Bridge.

They also talked excitedly of the wild rumors beginning to sweep London. People were saying the fire was no accident. All morning Farynor, the King's Baker, had told everyone who would listen that he had checked his ovens at midnight and they had been cold. This meant that someone must have started the fire in Pudding Lane! It might have been a Dutch plot to fire the City, and the French were probably involved, or even English Catholics!

Soon after Maid Jane brought in the lamprey pie, a neighbor burst into the Pepys's dining room. She was too upset to stay, as she was looking for her relatives. Their house on Fish Street Hill had burned down, and she was trying to locate them.

After dinner, Pepys and one of his guests went into the City to see how far the fire had advanced. Near the flames, they noticed the streets more crowded than ever. Families unable to rent carts had loaded their pots, pans, and kitchen stools on their backs. Mothers carried children in cribs. Cannon Street, where Pepys had seen the Lord Mayor earlier, was now being evacuated. Every householder who could, was moving his goods into streets farther away from the flames.

By now militia had been posted at strategic points near the perimeter of the fire, and despite the Lord Mayor's insistence that he needed no more troops, Charles had sent in the Horse Guards. Riding sleek horses, the scarlet-coated soldiers began patrolling the City, their presence helping to calm the excited citizenry. A detachment of thirty naval seamen also arrived in London. They suggested using gunpowder to pull down houses, but the idea was rejected as too dangerous, so they got to work instead with ladders, pickaxes, hooks, and chains.

Taswell, the Westminster School student, had reached the City and was walking toward the flames when he came across an angry mob looking for "the foreigners" who had started the fire. A Frenchman was spotted in the distance, and the mob rushed up. A blacksmith in the group ran over and hit the Frenchman with an iron bar, bloodying his head.

At Whitehall Palace, Charles II paced the floor of the royal bedchamber. A courier had just left after giving the latest report of the fire's advance. The news was not good, and at two-thirty in the afternoon Charles decided to go into the City. Summoning the Duke of York, Charles strode to the boat stairs where the royal barge was anchored. Sitting under a canopy of gold cloth supported by slender Corinthian columns, Charles ordered the captain to sail down the Thames.

When the barge reached the bend of the river, Charles's heart fell. The news of the fire, bad as it was, had not prepared him for what he saw. Along the riverbank, under a sky of black smoke, was a solid mass of fiery flames stretching from below the Steelyard to London Bridge.

As the royal barge docked, a crowd gathered, and Charles spotted Sir Richard Browne, an alderman and former Lord Mayor.

"The fire is spreading rapidly," Charles called over to Sir Richard. "Tell the Lord Mayor to pull down apace."

Later, Charles went ashore and climbed to the roof of a tall house. As he watched, tongues of flame shot out the windows of Watermen's Hall, home of one of London's most important City Companies.

Pepys by now was on the river again in a boat, heading back to Whitehall Palace. The Thames was full of lighters carrying household goods of fleeing Londoners. But, strangely, few were filled to capacity. While Pepys watched, one floated by carrying only a "pair of virginals," a 17th-century harpsichord.

Landing at the Whitehall boat stairs, Pepys met his wife Elizabeth and friends, and after a walk to St. James's Park they returned downstream, almost getting burned on the way by a "shower of firedrops." Live brands now were being wafted all over London, and houses far from the fire were becoming endangered.

By the time the Pepyses reached London Bridge, the air was full of smoke, and they stopped off at an alehouse on the Southwark side of the river. Until evening they stayed there, watching more of the City becoming engulfed by the "horrid, malicious flame." When they left, one fire front stretched almost three-quarters of a mile along the river, and another front had moved northward into the City more than one-quarter of a mile. As Pepys saw the buildings burn and heard the noise of the flames and the cracking of timbers, he wept.

With sad hearts, the Pepyses returned to their house on Seething Lane, and when they arrived, they found Tom Hayter, one of Pepys's clerks, standing outside with his clothes and household goods—all he could save when his house had burned. Pepys invited Hayter to stay at his house and store his goods there.

Later came Sir William Batten, Surveyor of the Navy, and Sir William Penn, Commissioner of the Navy, both of whom also lived in Seething Lane. They told Pepys they had arranged for carts to take away their furniture and possessions that night.

Pepys roused the maids and, with Tom Hayter's assistance, hurried to get his own furniture and goods into the garden so that they could be moved out more easily. In the moonlight, they all began hauling out mattresses, beds, rugs, and paintings. Pepys took his silver plate and iron chests down into the cellar for safety. He moved his bags of gold and his accounts to the Navy Office.

Not for many hours did Pepys stop work, but then, lighting a candelabra, he went upstairs and set it on a desk in his study. Sitting down, he picked up his diary and reached for his quill pen. Dipping it in ink, he began writing carefully in his cryptographic shorthand the events of this never-to-be-forgotten day:

September 2nd (*Lord's day*). Some of our maids sitting up late last night to get things ready against our feast to-day, Jane called us up about three in the morning, to tell us of a great fire they saw in the City. So I rose and . . .

II

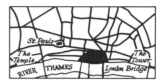

Monday, September 3, 1666

See the houses tumble, tumble, tumble from one end of the street to the other . . .

DAWN THAT MONDAY ushered in—if not for the fire—a beautiful morning. The sun spread its warm rays over London, and except for the wind ever blowing westward, the weather was autumn at its best.

At Whitehall Palace, Charles II had already risen. All night he had thought of nothing but the fire. From the palace windows, he, his ministers of state, and the Duke of York had looked toward London. They had not seen the City itself—it was too far—but they had watched the reddish glow in the sky and, now and then, the flames shooting high. When Charles had finally gone to bed, he had not slept.

The first courier to arrive in the morning brought discouraging news. Shortly after midnight, the Steelyard on the riverbank had been destroyed. Also burned down were hundreds—possibly even thousands—more homes as well as three more Company halls. Boar Head Tavern, once frequented by Shakespeare, was gone, and more important, London had lost its Post Office. Acting Postmaster John Hickes had been forced to abandon it. "When the violence of the fire is over, some place will be fixed upon for the general correspondence," he hastily wrote in a letter he circularized to all postmasters between London and Chester.

Fanned by the wind, flames were now advancing on two fronts—one moving north into the City, the other sweeping westward along the Thames.

Charles realized that Sir Thomas Bludworth and the other City officials were incapable of coping with the emergency. During the night he had formulated his plans, and he summoned his ministers and the Duke of York to give them his orders.

He, Charles II, was taking over complete authority in London. The Duke of York would be in command as his deputy, and a system of fire defenses was to be organized immediately. A series of fire posts would be set up around the fire's perimeter. Manned by one hundred civilians and commanded by a constable, each post would also have thirty foot soldiers and an officer, and three justices of the peace. Five pounds' worth of bread, cheese, and beer would be allotted to each post, and all men who served diligently would receive a one-shilling reward. Supervising the fire posts would be a special committee of Privy Council members and noblemen. They would report to Charles and the Duke of York regularly.

Charles also ordered that messages be rushed to the Lord Lieutenants of nearby counties asking them to send militia immediately to relieve the fire posts and help fight the fire.

After the conference, Charles had himself rowed down the Thames to London. Once ashore, he learned that three more churches had burned down, including St. Michael Paternoster Royal, where London's famous Mayor Dick Whittington was buried. The walls of the churches had

MILITIA PULLING DOWN HOUSES.

withstood the flames, but their wooden interiors had been completely gutted.

Not far from where the royal barge had docked was the market at Queenhithe, where fire fighters were stripping stalls and pulling down houses as fast as they could. The King encouraged the men for a half hour. But after he left, flames rushed in, suddenly leaped over the collapsed houses, and ignited the houses farther up the street. Now the fire had an unobstructed path all the way up the Thames riverfront almost to Fleet Ditch.

Samuel Pepys also had not slept well. After only a few hours, he was awakened by Sir William Batten. The Battens had already moved their valuables by cart to Bethnal Green, home of the wealthy merchant Sir William Rider. Pepys could now use the cart if he wanted. In his night-robe, Pepys got his iron chest from the cellar and piled it into the cart with his silver plate, important papers, and books. Then, still in his night-robe, he drove off through the streets toward the City wall.

Thousands of Londoners were fleeing, and when Pepys arrived at Bethnal Green, he was greeted by a weary Sir William Rider. The merchant had been up for hours receiving goods of friends. Pepys placed his valuables in the same room where the Battens and Penns had theirs. Then, relieved, he returned home.

Every avenue out of the City was now jammed. Those Londoners near the Thames crowded around the boat stairs, trying to rent boats. Others moved slowly northward through London's narrow, crooked streets. No longer did anyone try to seek safety for their goods in churches. Their only hope now, they realized, was to reach one of the open fields, like Moorfields, outside the City.

Through congested streets they pushed, some in elegant carriages, but most in carts or on foot, bringing what they could save from their homes. Streets became choked with traffic, and some were impassable. The one where a cart had overturned on Sunday was still blocked. On another, a dead horse lay stretched across the cobblestones.

It took hours to pass through the crowded City gates. Drivers cursed, women carrying babies screamed, and beggars waved their crutches in anger. Adding to the congestion were those entering London. No longer were they curious sightseers like the student Taswell. Now they were laborers and cartmen who came from the suburbs to get work moving families out of the City. Around the gates they crowded, shouting their rates, which were double and triple normal charges. But many householders were willing to pay even more.

Some cartmen were dishonest. With flames approaching, Taswell's father desperately tried to hire a cart to haul away his books and furniture. When he finally succeeded, he never saw the cartman or his furniture again.

When more militia arrived from nearby counties, much of the lawlessness was curbed. London's gates, however, were more congested than ever, and it was decided to close them to all but outgoing traffic.

With his valuables at Bethnal Green, Pepys now thought of getting to safety the furniture and household goods he had moved into his garden the previous night. There was room for them at Deptford, the royal dockyard on the Southwark side of the Thames farther down the river. All Pepys needed was a boat to take them there. With difficulty he hired one at the Tower of London, and soon he, his wife, and their maids were lugging the mattresses, bedsteads, and other furniture from the garden.

DRAYMEN & CARTERS HOLDING OUT FOR OUTRAGEOUS PRICES

By Monday afternoon flames had reached the stalls of the herb-and-fruit market on Gracechurch Street and were threatening Lombard Street. One of London's most picturesque streets, Lombard Street was the City's banking center. Here in their stout Elizabethan homes with casement windows, London's merchant-bankers conducted business. Over the doors of these homes swung gilded signs painted with symbols like the Unicorn, Grasshopper, and White Horse which distinguished their banking houses.

Most merchant-bankers had already fled. Almost twenty-four hours before, Robert Vyner, leading financier to the Crown, had moved out his papers and gold. At about two o'clock in the afternoon flames swept up Lombard Street, and one hour later all its beautiful homes were in flames.

The wind then drove the fire into Cornhill, the spacious shopping street where mercers and glovers sold their wares. With flames roaring at their backs, soldiers and civilians worked frantically pulling down houses on the south side of the street to prevent the fire from crossing over to the north side. There were two solidly built churches on the south side. If the fire fighters could pull down the adjoining timber houses in time, then . . .

A large crowd gathered to watch the pulling-down. To keep everyone at a distance, a company of Horse Guards rode in. With chain and hook, the embattled fire fighters pulled down the houses in time, but in the excitement no one picked up the timbers lying in the street. With a roar, the flames hit both churches, destroying them. Then, on the pathway formed by the timbers, the fire quickly crossed the street, and within a few hours, both sides of Cornhill were in ruins.

Water shortages hampered the fire fighting. With the Thames River water system out of commission, no water could be obtained from its pipes. Nor could much water be drawn from springs, since most had been dried up from a drought the previous summer. The New River water system, which covered most of the City not supplied by the Thames system, was also inadequate. When it was built, engineers had installed water cocks at specified points so that in case of fire large quantities of water could be drawn. But panicky Londoners—to fill their leathern buckets more quickly—had made dozens of cuts in the system's wooden pipes. As a result, the pipes were like sieves, and water only trickled out in the places it was so desperately needed.

By mid afternoon, an immense curtain of smoke hung over London, and everyone had trouble seeing the sun. Since Sunday, the burning warehouses along the Thames had been sending upward billowing clouds of black smoke. Also aflame now were the warehouses back from the river where barrels of cordials and brandy were stored. When the sun did peek through, it looked "red like blood." Miles from London, travelers noticed the sky's unusual color, and one observer reported seeing "sunbeams dancing with a strange dim red light."

Across the river near Deptford was Sayes Court, an estate whose gardens were considered among the most beautiful in England. Here lived John Evelyn, an aristocrat who wrote books, dabbled in architecture, and served as His Majesty's Commissioner for the Sick and Wounded Prisoners in the Dutch War. Dining with his wife and sons, Evelyn noticed a column of smoke rising from the direction of London. At first Evelyn thought the smoke had come from London's soap factories, breweries, and lime burners.

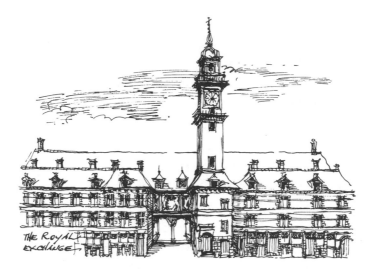

THE ROYAL EXCHANGE

Shortly after the Restoration, he had impressed Charles with his book *Fumifugium,* which explained how the City's industries were polluting its air.

But soon Evelyn realized that London was afire. Calling for his coach, he drove his family to Southwark to get a closer look at "the dismall spectacle." Flames were now advancing to the heart of the City. St. Paul's high on a hill to the west was as yet unthreatened. But the Royal Exchange was in danger. Modeled after the stock-exchange building in Amsterdam, the Royal Exchange had been donated to London almost a century before by Sir Thomas Gresham, a wealthy merchant. A large square building, four stories high, it had a tall stone clock tower topped by a weathervane in the shape of a grasshopper—Gresham's sign. Inside the Royal Exchange was a spacious courtyard around which ran a cloistered walk. Here, under a roof supported by marble columns, London's merchants strolled, conducting their transactions. Set in niches along the wall were statues of England's kings and of Gresham himself.

Around the outside of the Royal Exchange were several hundred shops and offices, and the flames hit these first. Rising rapidly, they blazed up the stairways into the upstairs galleries, and within an hour, swept into the courtyard, enveloping it in a massive fiery sheet. For hours the Royal Exchange burned, until finally its walls crashed with a mighty roar. When the smoldering ruins settled, all that remained of one of England's greatest buildings was a single marble pillar and the tower's seared skeleton. All the statues had fallen and shattered except one—Sir Thomas Gresham's.

Frightened and angry, Londoners were more and more unwilling to believe that the fire had started naturally. Most assumed it originated from a sinister plot, and such thinking was not illogical. Several months before, after unsuccessfully trying to catch Dutch Admiral De Ruyter, the English fleet had sailed to the island of Vlie off the coast of Holland, and fired the port as well as 160 Dutch merchantmen in the harbor.

Many thought the fire of London stemmed from Dutch retaliation. Others believed the French, England's traditional enemy, had assisted the Dutch. Still others put the blame on English Papists who, many Protestants believed, would stop at nothing to return England to Catholicism.

Seeking the "perpetrators" of London's terrible fire, mobs armed themselves with spits, bread staffs, and swords, and roamed the streets. Avoiding the militia and Horse Guards, they attacked anyone they thought suspect.

Usually this meant foreigners, and most foreigners still in London wisely stayed indoors. Many of those who happened to be in the streets were jailed by magistrates for their own protection. But dozens of incidents occurred. The student Taswell came upon a mob looting and burning the shop of a French painter. Another Frenchman was surrounded by an angry mob in Moorfields. He was carrying a chest containing fluffy objects that resembled the combustible fireballs used in warfare. The Frenchman insisted that they were only tennis balls. When his accusers looked more closely, they found that he was telling the truth.

Not even Londoners were immune from the mob. A widow was caught fleeing into Moorfields, hiding what seemed to be fireballs under her apron. She was beaten severely until it was discovered that the fluffy objects were baby chicks—all she had been able to save of her possessions.

The Duke of York had the responsibility for preventing looting and attacks on foreigners. All day, as he galloped around to the fire posts encouraging civilians, troops, and navymen to keep pulling down buildings, he tried to prevent such incidents. Riding near Westminster, he came upon a mob gathering around a Dutch baker named Cornelius Riedveldt. Men and women were screaming that Riedveldt was trying to set Westminster afire. The baker protested. London needed bread in the emergency; he had just lit his ovens to bake some. To save Riedveldt's life, the Duke of York ordered him taken to prison.

On and on Londoners struggled to save themselves and their city. Neighbors helped neighbors. Churchwardens rushed into churches to save the parish plate and registers only to find their own homes in flames when they returned. Some citizens organized fire-fighting squads on their own. The Dean of Westminster marched the West-

minster School students two-and-one-half miles to London
and then another mile and a half through the City. Their
mission was to save St. Dunstan-in-the-East, whose lead-
covered steeple was the second highest in London. For
hours, students fetched water in buckets and poured it on
the church and surrounding houses. When flames finally
swept up the street, St. Dunstan-in-the-East was defaced,
but not destroyed.

Later, another dramatic act of personal fire fighting
took place at Leadenhall. A big lead-roofed building with
battlemented walls, Leadenhall served as a market,
granary, and armory, as well as headquarters for the East
India Company. For hours, exhausted fire fighters had been
pulling down nearby houses and were about to give up
when an unknown municipal official flung a hatful of gold
coins among them. With renewed effort, the men returned
to pulling down. When the flames finally reached Leadenhall, only its western front was damaged.

By Monday evening, the London fire was so bright,
the night seemed like day. There was also a fearful rattling
noise which Reverend Thomas Vincent described as "a
thousand chariots beating on the stones." Reverend Thomas
wrote later that never in his wildest fantasies had he imag-
ined anything as terrible. He saw entire streets burning as
if "fired from great forges" and "houses tumble, tumble,
tumble from one end of the street to the other, with a great
crash, leaving their foundations open to the view of the
heavens."

The fire front along the Thames now reached as far
west as Baynard's Castle, the ancient Norman fortress near
Fleet Ditch. Flames raced across the castle's entire front
and then shot out the windows, casting eerie reflections on

the water where burning timbers floated by.

John Evelyn, returning to Southwark that evening, saw Baynard's Castle burning. Even though he was on the other side of the river, the air was so hot and inflamed that he had trouble breathing. The sky was artificially bright for forty miles around, and over London it reminded Evelyn of the top of a burning oven.

As Evelyn watched in horror, flames leapt from house to house. He heard men and women shrieking, and houses and churches crashing down. Like Pepys, a friend and fellow member of the recently founded Royal Society, Evelyn kept a diary. That night at Sayes Court, he could hardly compose his thoughts as he started to write.

> I left it . . . burning, a resemblance to Sodom . . . [its] ruines looked like the ruines of Troy. . . . London was, but is no more. . . . Oh, the miserable and calamitous spectacle. . . . God grant mine eyes never behold the like again.

At Whitehall Palace, sitting by a lattice window in her palace chamber, looking at the orange-red sky, was Catherine of Braganza, Charles's faithful wife. Daughter of the Queen Regent of Portugal, she had brought Tangiers, Bombay, and three million livres as a dowry when she came to England four years before to marry Charles.

The Earl of Clarendon was announced. Now Lord Chancellor, as Edward Hyde he had been Charles's mentor and guardian during all the years of exile on the Continent.

"It is spreading," Catherine said, turning from the window.

Clarendon shook his head. The King, he said, had

been out fighting the fire since early morning.

"After this, my Lord, no one can speak ill of Charles," Catherine said.

The Earl of Clarendon agreed. He was about to leave when Catherine asked him one more question. Would Charles's efforts be enough to save London?

Clarendon explained that despite what his enemies said, Charles had always been a man of great courage.

"And," he added, "it is this courage that has given us victory so far over the Dutch."

At the end of the day, as at the beginning of the day, the fire was advancing on two fronts, one westward along the river, the other northward into the City. Late Monday night at Stocks Market, where London's fishmongers and butchers had their stalls, the two fronts met. The stalls vanished immediately in the flames, and so did the nearby compter, one of the Sheriff's many prisons in the City. Its prisoners had been released earlier and told to head for Moorfields.

There was still only one casualty from the fire—Farynor's maidservant. But the loss in property had mounted tremendously. Hundreds more houses had fallen to the flames, and many more churches like St. Swithin's. More Company Halls like Salters Hall and Paynter-Stainers Hall had been destroyed too. So, also, had more shops like the grocery and apothecary stores in Bucklersbury, which sent strange odors into the air after catching fire.

Pepys and his wife were exhausted after their trying day. Eating leftovers for supper, they went over to the Navy Office in Seething Lane to sleep. Since all their furniture was now at Deptford, Pepys borrowed a quilt from Will Hewer, his confidential secretary.

As Monday midnight approached, families still fled the City, crowding the gates, stumbling into the suburbs with their goods on their backs. Out in Moorfields, and farther north in Finsbury Fields, thousands of Londoners were now camped under the stars, their possessions beside them. Overhead, the smoke was thick, and the air heated. Bewildered and exhausted, they looked back and saw flames leaping high over the City's ancient walls. They heard the explosions and the crashes of falling walls. A few clutched in their hands the official *London Gazette* published that morning. Before the *Gazette* had abruptly suspended operations because of the flames' advance, it managed to print twelve lines about the fire: "It still continues with great violence," the brief article began.

III

Tuesday, September 4, 1666

It's at Barking Church
at the foot of our lane . . .

DURING THE NIGHT, the wind had increased in velocity. Half of London had now been leveled, and flames were approaching the ancient City walls at Ludgate and Newgate. Once through and across the Fleet Ditch, they could sweep unchecked into the western Liberties.

Charles with the Duke of York had been making the rounds of the fire posts since early morning. Thousands more homes had been reported destroyed, and dozens more Company halls and churches. Burned down was St. John the Evangelist, whose parish had been miraculously spared during the Plague. Also destroyed was All Hallows, Bread Street, but not before churchwardens had saved the register recording the baptism of John Milton.

A report came in that Cheapside was threatened. The showcase of London, Cheapside was the one surviving market street from the Middle Ages. Only six years before, while his subjects cheered, Charles had ridden down Cheapside in his coronation procession, passing between house fronts decorated with tapestries. Lining Cheapside's southern side was Goldsmiths' Row; its two dozen houses and shops were considered the most beautiful in England. A London Sheriff had built them a century before, and they were famous for their gilded, carved decorations of gold-smith arms—"wildmen" riding beasts.

A stone-built chapel was momentarily blocking the flames moving on Cheapside from the east, but another fire front was moving up from the south. Joining at the chapel, the flames destroyed it, and then crashed into Cheapside. Soon beautiful Goldsmiths' Row was in flames. Mermaid Tavern, immortalized by Ben Jonson and Shakespeare, was destroyed. St. Mary-le-Bow was left roofless.

As Charles rode through London that morning, he carried over his shoulder a purse containing one hundred gold guineas. As he galloped by the fire fighters, he tossed out coins to encourage them. Unmindful of the dangers from falling timbers or a possible assassin lurking in the crowd, Charles and the Duke of York often dismounted. Ankle deep in mud, their lace cuffs dripping, their faces blackened with dirt, they lent a hand with the spades, and joined lines passing leathern water buckets.

Pulling-down was still the only effective fire-fighting method, but shortages had developed of fire hooks, ladders, rope, and axes. The Duke of York dispatched orders to adjoining counties. Troops were not needed now, but work-

KING CHARLES ANKLE DEEP IN MUD ON THE BUCKET PASSING LINE..

men with tools. Londoners too were ordered to contribute
equipment. A man named Starkey furnished thirteen dozen
pails and sixty brooms.

Pepys had also risen at dawn. The sky seemed more
full of smoke and flames than ever. His muscles ached, but
he still had some odds and ends to move. Waking his wife
Elizabeth and the maids, he walked them over to the
Tower of London, where again, because of the crowds, he
had trouble renting a lighter. But finally he hired one, and
back to Seething Lane they hurried to haul away the remaining boxes and hampers.

Flames were now pushing northward from Cheapside
into the streets leading to Guildhall. Constructed in the
Middle Ages, this solid stone-walled building with its great
hall was the seat of London's municipal administration.
Here the Lord Mayor, sheriffs, and aldermen had their
offices, and in stone vaults below were the City's records—
Coroner's rolls and wills dating back to the thirteenth
century.

When flames neared Guildhall, no attempt was made
to remove the records: they were too bulky. Fire hit the
galleries first, flooding them completely. Then it burst
through the windows and roof. Guildhall's flooring and
most of its interior were quickly destroyed, but its stone
walls stood, glowing strangely like a bright shining coal.
"A palace of gold, or a great building of tarnished brass,"
one observer described the phenomenon. The next day,
when the heat finally subsided, Guildhall's walls were still
standing, and even part of its roof. The irreplaceable records in its stone vaults had not been touched.

From Guildhall, the flames separated into two fronts.
One moved westward to Aldersgate. A heavy stone tower

built in the City wall, Aldersgate had a narrow gateway over which was erected a large equestrian relief statue of King James I, Charles's grandfather. All morning the fire advanced on Aldersgate, and by afternoon flames burst through the gateway. But thirty houses beyond the gate, the fire stopped.

The other front from Guildhall moved northward. In its path was Coopers Hall, whose members made London's barrels. That morning they had assembled for their monthly meeting. But when the flames approached, they turned instead to moving out all the Company's silver plate, pewter, linen, and records.

Coopers Hall fell victim to the flames. The fire front then moved farther northward to Cripplegate. Before the Norman Conquest, Cripplegate had been a recognized begging place for cripples, and now—like other City gates—it had a compter where debtors and others convicted of minor felonies were held.

For almost forty-eight hours flames had raged around Cripplegate, but the gate was not breached. Here for the first time gunpowder was used to collapse buildings. This was the idea that had been suggested on Sunday by the small naval detachment sent in to help.

While Charles and the Duke of York watched, the seamen went to work, putting barrels of powder in the houses to be demolished and linking the barrels up with a long fuse. The explosion lifted the houses off the ground, and they collapsed with a crash.

Everyone in London now had trouble breathing. Entire streets were being destroyed in just a few hours. So rapid was the fire's advance, the flames arrived before anyone realized they were near. Workmen to help with the

Blowing up Houses

moving and pulling-down were at a premium. Rewards of a hundred pounds were not uncommon to get laborers to apply their hooks and chains more quickly. But some home-owners were niggardly even now. Sir Richard Browne paid only four pounds to the men who risked their lives pulling out of his house an iron chest containing ten thousand pounds. Alderman Starling distributed only two shillings sixpence to all the workmen who saved his house. And when they finished clearing away his rubbish from the path of the flames, he began quarreling with them and com-plained they had come only to steal.

It was now almost impossible to hire a cart to move household goods out of the City. Draymen kept raising their prices until forty and fifty pounds for a cart was not un-usual. One wealthy Londoner paid four hundred pounds; later on, prices soared until charges equal to half the entire value of the goods moved were not considered exorbitant.

With axles creaking, carts piled high with furniture moved through the congested streets toward London's gates. Shopkeepers tried to move out their stocks. Alehouse owners even trundled wine casks over the cobblestones. Many streets were blocked. Detours were frequent, and troops stopped traffic at some streets, ordering those fleeing to take other routes. The sick and aged were still being carried in beds, and women still cried as they left their homes behind.

The exodus continued all day. Outside the City walls, Moorfields and Finsbury Fields were crowded with the homeless, and refugees now moved on to Islington, Highgate, and even St. Giles. Charles had stationed Trained Bands at these locations to prevent theft and looting. He had also ordered schools, churches, and public buildings in

CONFUSION & JAMS AT
THE CITY GATES

the areas to receive people's property for safekeeping.

By Tuesday afternoon a stream of refugees jammed the high roads leading out of London. Hundreds had collapsed by the roadside, too weary to go on. Rumbling by them constantly were carts, bringing goods from the City and returning for more. By this time the need for additional carts was so great that the order forbidding carts to enter London had been rescinded.

No matter how many miles away a Londoner got, he could hear the roaring flames and the crack of houses exploded by gunpowder. When he looked back, he could see the City wreathed in flames, and burning embers flying through the air beneath low clouds of sulfurous smoke.

By late afternoon, having finished moving the last of his possessions, Pepys returned to his home on Seething Lane and nervously watched the fire approach. With Sir William Penn, he walked several times to the end of the street to see how close the flames were. On one trip a man ran up and said someone had just died near the Tower of London "frightted by the fire."

The wind was of gale proportions now, and light debris was swirling around, being deposited with soot and ashes over the City's houses and gardens. Five miles way in Kensington, sparks and also bits of paper, plasterwork, and linen danced in the sky, blown from London by the wind. "You would have thought . . . it had been Doomsday," one man wrote. At Windsor Great Park, Lady Carteret saw scraps of paper fall from the sky. Picking one up, she read the words: "Time is it is done."

Disorder mounted in London. Many poor people, their possessions gone, hovered around the fire's outskirts, looking for goods to steal. Panic also heightened. The gunpowder explosions prompted more wild rumors. One was that a Dutch fleet was moving up the Thames, and Tower of London cannon were trying to beat it off. Others excitedly said that a French army of fifty thousand troops was marching on London.

Mobs still roamed the City, searching for foreigners and Papists. At the Temple, a man was arrested for carrying what seemed like combustible material. At Nag's Head Tavern, a suspicious-looking European was seized. A screaming woman told a magistrate that the lantern the European was carrying contained gunpowder.

On Seething Lane, Sir William Batten was preparing to leave the City. Pepys and Sir William Penn found him digging a pit in his garden for his wine, the only possession he had not moved. "The jostling in a cart would ruin it," Batten said. "It is better to bury it here and take a chance on its not being molested."

RETALIATION AGAINST FOREIGNERS & STRANGERS

Pepys thought the pit a good place to store the Navy Office records. Could he put them in the pit too?

Batten agreed, and Pepys went to get the records.

More troops arrived Tuesday afternoon, and fifty more naval seamen. But the wind still swept westward, and flames advanced faster than ever. Now they approached the alleys and streets leading to St. Paul's Cathedral, mightiest building in all England. For days, homeowners and shopkeepers had been moving goods and possessions into its spacious churchyard. Here London's mercers had stored hundreds of bolts of cloth, and London's booksellers, thousands of book volumes which they had hauled from their stalls in nearby Paternoster Row.

One by one the buildings below St. Paul's had caught fire: the Royal College of Surgeons, Stationers Hall, and St. Paul's School.

Still, St. Paul's Cathedral seemed in no danger. So massive was its construction, so heavy its stone, St. Paul's seemed impervious to any destructive force. Even so, the booksellers decided to move their books from the churchyard to a safer place. Underground, in the crypt of St. Paul's, was the parish church of St. Faith's. Its ceiling was St. Paul's floor. Here the booksellers brought their books; each man's stock was separated and identified with a number so that after the fire it could be easily brought up and separated. The booksellers assured themselves that no safer place existed in London. Even if St. Paul's burned, St. Faith's, being underground, was protected. Also, St. Faith was the patron saint of booksellers.

On the Thames, flames had advanced from Baynard's Castle to Fleet Ditch. Little more than a bricked-over sewer, Fleet Ditch was lined with weatherboard shacks,

crudely constructed with tacks. Here London's poorest
working population lived.

The day before, a suggestion had been made to tear
down the shacks to prevent the flames from spreading farther into the Liberties. But, with the fire then far away, the
idea had been rejected. Now, too late, troops and civilians
—anyone who could be commanded, threatened, or bribed
—were moved into the area to begin tearing down the
shacks.

In the midst of the frantic pulling-down, flames suddenly crashed through Ludgate, the City's most western
gate, and ignited the houses outside the wall. The fire
fighters by Fleet Ditch fell back. As they did, sparks and
embers from the burning houses set afire the shacks they
were pulling down. By Tuesday evening, the Liberties as
far west as Shoe Lane were afire, and flames had reached
the smelly breweries and tanneries farther north.

Next, flames reached Newgate, the western gate just
north of Ludgate. The prisoners from Newgate's compter
had been released several hours before. They had been
marched to Southwark, and in the confusion, many of the
worst criminals had escaped.

That morning flames had destroyed the stalls of Newgate market where tripe sellers and butchers sold their
meat. Now they hit the gate itself. Newgate was damaged,
but its stout masonry held. Even so, some flames got
through, and headed north in the direction of Smithfield,
but near Cock Lane they were stopped. Spared was St.
Bartholomew's Hospital. Many patients here were wounded
prisoners, and all day, John Evelyn, His Majesty's Commissioner for the Sick and Wounded Prisoners, had been near
the hospital helping to blow up houses.

By Tuesday evening only two areas in London re-

fire advancing over the rooftops

mained untouched by the flames. One was in the northeast, where Seething Lane was. Flames had advanced considerably slower in this direction because of the east wind. On the river, they had not gotten much farther than the Custom House, and in the interior, they were still several streets away from the Navy Office.

Yet the fire was advancing, and Pepys was worried. As he saw it, unless action was taken, the Navy Office would be lost. Sitting in his garden with Sir William Penn, Pepys proposed sending for men from the royal dockyards to pull down the houses at the end of Seething Lane.

Penn agreed it was a good idea, but permission was needed from the Duke of York. Pepys went inside and wrote a letter to Sir William Coventry, the Duke's private secretary. "Pray please let me have . . . at whatever hour it is, what his R.H. [Royal Highness] directions are in this answer." No reply was received, but Penn that night went down to the royal dockyards and arranged to bring up the men the following morning.

The other untouched area was St. Paul's Cathedral. For hours this tremendous cathedral had been surrounded by a sea of flames. Yet, "as if by Divine Providence," its great tower rose unburned above the swirling smoke and flames. Two decades after the Normans conquered England, construction had been started on St. Paul's. Built on the site of an ancient Saxon church, it had been first designed in Norman style, later as twin abbey churches. As centuries passed, many additions had been made. A huge central tower was erected. Later, over this, a timber spire was built, giving the tower a height of 245 feet. St. Paul's length was 585 feet.

Lightning had struck St. Paul's tower in the fourteenth and fifteenth centuries, and both times the tower was rebuilt. But the tower was struck again in 1561, and this time it was capped with a low, pyramid-shaped roof. Famed architect Inigo Jones had added a beautiful portico with fourteen Corinthian columns, each more than sixty feet tall.

In recent years St. Paul's had been shamefully neglected. During the Commonwealth, Cromwell's soldiers had removed lead from the cathedral's roof to use in making water pipe. Also, they had sold the scaffolding erected by Charles I to make repairs. At one point, soldiers had even ridden horses up the cathedral's steps and used its interior as a cavalry barracks. Small shops had been allowed to operate between the buttresses of the choir. Printers had installed their presses in vaults west of the crypt. Londoners, too lazy to walk around St. Paul's, took shortcuts through its nave.

Even worse was St. Paul's physical deterioration. Fumes from coal smoke had disintegrated its stonework. The weight of the lead covering its roofs—some six acres in area—had spread its walls, and the tower no longer stood straight.

Earlier in 1666, Charles had appointed a commission to draw up plans for St. Paul's restoration. John Evelyn was a member. So was a brilliant thirty-four-year-old Oxford professor of astronomy and geometry named Christopher Wren. He had not yet designed a completed building, but his designs had already won recognition among other architects—all of whom were "amateurs" since architecture had not yet become a profession. At John Evelyn's suggestion, the King had appointed Wren Deputy Surveyor of His Majesty's Works, a position which made him responsible (under the Surveyor) for the architecture of all royal and government buildings.

The commission had erected a scaffolding to start repairs on St. Paul's, and a week before the fire started, it had inspected the great cathedral in order to present a complete renovation scheme to the King.

Now on Tuesday, September 4, 1666, St. Paul's stood almost alone in the burning city—a symbol of impregnability. Then, about eight o'clock that evening a bookseller, standing in the cathedral's churchyard, saw a live brand land on St. Paul's tower on a board that had patched up an area where lead had broken off. Immediately the tower blazed up, and within minutes, flames began shooting from St. Paul's in every direction. Timbers under the cathedral's roof caught fire, melting the lead overhead. As "snow running before the sun," it began to drip and run down both inside and outside St. Paul's. Roof timbers crashed into the nave and choir. Huge chunks of masonry tumbled down, smashing through the floor and breaking into the vaults of St. Faith's below. The thousands of books stored there blazed up in an inferno. Huge jets of flame shot out the cathedral's windows.

The intense heat peeled and stripped great flakes of stone from the cathedral's walls. Slabs of masonry, some as heavy as one hundred pounds, exploded, and were hurled like cannonballs from the cathedral. Molten lead flowed over the broken tombs and effigies on the cathedral's floor, and into St. Faith's. Forming a stream, the lead ran down the hill, making St. Paul's pavement glow red-hot.

Steaming debris cluttered the area and kept everyone hundreds of feet away from the burning cathedral. A large crowd of stunned onlookers gathered nearby, and Charles and the Duke of York galloped up. Sadly they watched as the sides of St. Paul's gave way, revealing a gigantic cauldron of flames inside.

Taswell, the Westminster School student, was more than a mile away. Yet, from the light of blazing St. Paul's, he had no trouble—even at night—reading the fine print of a small edition of Terence he carried in his pocket. John Evelyn wrote in his diary: "Nothing but ye Almighty power of God was able to stop them [the flames] for vaine was the help of man."

While St. Paul's burned (as it would for days) the fire continued its horrible advance. Even in the northwest, where flames had never made much progress, it now began to spread faster. To the west, much of the Liberties beyond the City wall was afire, and westward along the river flames were also still advancing.

ST. PAULS BURNING

On the Thames, farther up from the spot where the Fleet Ditch flowed in, was Bridewell, once a Tudor palace, now a "house of correction." In some of its unused space, four thousand quarters of the City's grain was stored. When flames struck, the heat became so intense that the dead in nearby graves burned.

The fire now moved farther up the river to Whitefriars, or Alsatia, the run-down area where London's criminals lived. Its onetime mansions had become dilapidated and were now crowded, dirty tenements. Whitefriars had hundreds of cheap taverns and brothels, and swarming through its streets were highwaymen, escaped felons, and cutpurses.

The houses here blazed up like matchwood, and then the fire rushed on westward up the river to the Temple, the district for London's lawyers. In the twelfth century, before they marched off to fight in the Crusades, the Knights Templars had occupied this area, and then the property had passed to the Knights Hospitallers of St. John, who leased it to professors of law. When these teachers took on pupils as resident students, they started England's first law university.

Most Temple lawyers were on vacation, but those still on the grounds had taken steps to protect its numerous buildings—the Middle Temple, the Inner Temple, and the many courts, gardens, and inns like Gray's, Sergeants', and Clifford's. A brick wall separated the Temple from Whitefriars, but even so, sailors from the fleet had been sent in with barrels of gunpowder to blow up the surrounding shops and houses, and engineers had been hired at one sovereign each to supervise the demolishing.

But at eleven that evening Charles and the Duke of

York were summoned. Flames had broken over the wall and were destroying a row of brick houses on the other side. Farther westward were wooden houses, and the two royal brothers ordered these pulled down to save the Temple's other buildings.

The Temple also faced danger from another fire front moving south from Fleet Ditch. One lawyer found himself almost surrounded by flames. Desperately trying to save his law books, he ran to the river, but was unable to hire a boatman. Then he rushed back to Fleet Street, which formed the northern boundary of the Temple's property, but no cart was available there. Finally he gave up his books to the flames and concentrated on saving himself.

The Inner Temple caught fire, and the law libraries of

THE LAWYER WHO TRIED TO SAVE HIS BOOKS

hundreds of lawyers as well as their papers and chests of money were in flames. Destroyed also were copies of the wills and estates of thousands of Londoners. The church of the Knights Templars survived and also the Inner Temple Hall, but the rest of the Inner Temple was ruined.

At its height, the wind now whipped with unparalleled fury across burning London. Fleet Street westward turned into the road to Westminster, and the old timber houses lining both sides of the narrow cobblestoned highway quickly disappeared in smoke. Alarm now spread to the Strand—the area between London and Westminster where great estates fronted the Thames. Many residents had already cleared their houses of furniture and sent it up the Thames by barge. But others who had delayed now panicked, fleeing frantically into the street, leaving everything behind.

At Whitehall Palace, the Court was in confusion. Because of the flames advancing down Fleet Street, all Westminster, including Whitehall, was endangered. Charles had already ordered the houses blown up around Somerset House, where his mother, Queen Mother Henrietta Maria, lived. The Duke of York was there now, preparing to move her out the following morning. To help protect Whitehall, Charles commanded Scotland Yard's new buildings to be unroofed.

Then, suddenly, at eleven that night, when the great fire was at its worst, the wind began to fall.

The fire was by no means over; it would continue for days. But the wind's slackening meant it would no longer spread so rapidly. The realization of this recharged the fire fighters' sagging spirits. At the Temple, the soldiers and civilians pulling down with hooks and tackle were almost ready to give up. But when the wind fell, they turned back to the pulling down with renewed effort.

In the east, by Tuesday night flames were approaching the Tower of London. Panic had momentarily seized the fire fighters earlier when someone remembered that all the Navy's gunpowder was stored in the Tower. If it ever caught fire, it could blow London Bridge sky high, sink every vessel in the Thames, and devastate the area for miles around. Luckily, the gunpowder had been moved out a few hours before and taken down the river. Also, the million pounds' worth of gold and jewelry deposited in the Tower the day before by London's goldsmiths had been moved up the Thames to Whitehall Palace.

Seething Lane was only a few streets away from the Tower, and Pepys had been anxiously watching the flames advance. He and Sir William Penn had dug a pit for their wine as Sir William Batten had done, and Pepys also put in his Parmesan cheese. With cousins, they ate supper in the Navy Office, their fare being a shoulder of mutton purchased from a cookshop. There were "no napkins or anything," but despite the sad circumstances, they all managed to be merry.

During supper, Pepys kept going into the garden to see how fast the flames were advancing. The sky looked horrible. As Pepys reported, it was as if the entire heavens were on fire and "just as if it were at us." It was "enough to put us out of our wits."

Down by the Tower of London, Pepys saw fire fighters blowing up houses with gunpowder. At first the noise frightened people, but soon everyone noticed that it was stopping "the fire where it was done, it bringing down the houses to the ground in the same places they stood, and then it was easy to quench what little fire was in it, though it kindled nothing almost."

Back in the Navy Office, Pepys was too exhausted to write in his diary. But he did pen a letter to his father in Brampton, even though he knew the letter would not get there because there was no Post Office. Weary, his feet so sore he could hardly stand, Pepys lay down on Will Hewer's quilt.

At two in the morning, Elizabeth woke him up. "The fire," she said excitedly. "It's at Barking Church at the bottom of our lane."

IV

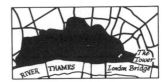

Wednesday-Friday, September 5-7, 1666

The saddest sight of desolation that I ever saw . . .

IMMEDIATELY AFTER HIS wife Elizabeth gave the alarm early Wednesday morning, Pepys dressed and hurried down to the end of Seething Lane to All Hallows Barking. Flames were beginning to lick up the church's walls, and Pepys decided it was time to flee London. Collecting his gold from the Navy Office, he hurried with Elizabeth and Will Hewer to the boat stairs at the Tower of London, and hired a waterman to take them to the royal dockyard at Woolwich. A little further down than Deptford, Woolwich had lodgings where Elizabeth had lived during the worst months of the Plague.

As the waterman rowed them down the Thames, they noticed a heavy cloud of reddish smoke overhead, and once at Woolwich, they still felt in the heart of the flames. Pepys discovered that the gates were shut and no guards were present. As secretary to the Navy Board he was worried. Could it be true that the French were marching on London? Is that where the guards had gone?

But finally some guards turned up, and Pepys led Elizabeth and Will Hewer to the lodgings. Locking up the gold in one room, he ordered them never to leave the gold alone. If one had to go out, the other was to stay.

On the way back to London, Pepys stopped off at Deptford to make sure his household goods there were still secure. Then, at seven o'clock, his boat bumped again at the Tower of London dock. Pepys was sure the Navy Office had burned down by now, but hesitated to ask anyone. However, much to his surprise, the fire had not advanced much farther than when he had left. The naval dockyard-men brought in by Sir William Penn had blown up a wine-shop and warehouse at the foot of Seething Lane, and the flames had been checked. All Hallows Barking church was still intact, although the clock face on its tower and its walls were damaged.

After a quick look at his own house to make sure it had not been touched, Pepys climbed to the top of the All Hallows Barking steeple. Before his eyes stretched "the saddest sight of desolation that I ever saw." Although the wind had subsided, much of the City was still burning. Everywhere Pepys looked, he saw great fires, burning houses, and smoking warehouses. Tongues of flames still shot skyward from St. Paul's, and much of the Liberties were still burning, as were many streets around Cripplegate, the gate in the north of London.

From Whitehall Palace that morning, Charles II was directing the final fire-fighting efforts. Meeting with his Privy Council, he briefed them on the strategy and assigned them to stations. One station was assigned to John Evelyn, who had been summoned to assist in the pulling-down operations. Before Evelyn left, Charles called him aside. The sky black with smoke, Charles said, reminded him of Evelyn's smoke nuisance description in *Fumifugium*.

The slackening of the wind had given London renewed hope, and as the cracks of gunpowder explosions shattered the air, the fire fighters pitched in with newfound energy. Charles and the Duke of York spent most of Wednesday at Cripplegate, one of the few areas where flames were still of major proportions. Reappearing here was Sir Thomas Bludworth, London's Lord Mayor. Under his supervision a dozen houses were pulled down.

Out in Moorfields, many of those who saw the fire begin to subside came back into the City to help with the fire fighting. Those who stayed started to build makeshift shelters, and tents, huts, and hovels soon dotted the fields. Many of those camping out had only the clothes they wore, and only a few had cooking utensils. Wealthy families who several days before had lived in luxurious homes surrounded by servants now found themselves reduced to "extreamist misery and poverty."

Charles now turned his attention to the several hundred thousand Londoners in the field, and he issued two royal proclamations for their relief. The first ensured an adequate food supply. Several days before, Charles had ordered biscuits sent in from the Navy to Moorfields, but most went uneaten. Even though the refugees were hungry, they could not stomach the hard Navy fare. Now Charles ordered large quantities of food—mostly bread—sent in from the adjoining counties. These provisions were to be distributed daily at central points throughout the few unburned areas of the city.

For those who had fled farther north, Charles ordered the establishment of temporary markets in locations convenient to them. "We have taken care to secure the said markets in safety," his proclamation said, "and to prevent all disturbances by the refusal of payment for goods and otherwise."

Charles's second proclamation ordered cities and towns outside London to receive refugees "without contradiction." Churches, schools, chapels, and other public places were to receive the household goods of these displaced Londoners. Also, any artisans among those who had fled were to be allowed to ply their trade without restriction by local guild regulations. The King pledged his word that, once the emergency had passed, none of these homeless Londoners would become a burden on the town that took them in.

After lunching on an unappetizing piece of cold meat at Sir William Penn's, Pepys with friends of Penn took a walk through the still burning City. Street after street they found completely leveled, and the Royal Exchange was "a sad sight." Pepys found many people in Moorfields aimlessly carrying their belongings to and fro. Others simply sat beside their possessions, too dazed to move. How fortunate it was for these homeless, Pepys realized, that the weather was not inclement.

After stopping at a tavern for ale and later begrudgingly paying twopence for a loaf of bread that normally cost a penny, Pepys passed the house of his cousin by marriage. Not even its foundations were standing. Then he walked by the ruins of the Royal Exchange again, just as some men were pulling a cat from a hole in a chimney wall. Its hair was burned off, but it was still alive. Farther on, at the site of a destroyed Company hall, Pepys found a piece of glass that had melted and been buckled by the fire. Picking it up, he put it in his pocket as a souvenir.

A few fresh outbreaks still occurred throughout Wednesday. Sparks in the air ignited some houses not far from Seething Lane, and at Shoe Lane in the Liberties, flames flared up briefly. One last violent outbreak also occurred at Cripplegate, sending a red glare over ruined London.

By eleven o'clock that evening the Duke of York, who had slept little since Sunday, decided the fire was enough under control for him to go to bed. But no sooner had he returned to Whitehall Palace than messengers arrived with news that fire had broken out again in the Temple. Summoning his horse, the Duke arrived at the Temple's gate on Fleet Street to find a large crowd outside, but no fire fighters inside. Those in charge of the Temple had refused to admit anyone for fear of looting.

The Duke, a Bencher of the Temple himself, ordered the gates opened, and escorted the fire fighters inside. The new fire had started when sparks from still smoldering Temple houses had gusted over to some buildings near the Inner Temple. To save the Hall, the Duke saw no recourse but to blow up the Paper House in the courtyard. The Duke

Temple Bar Burning

ordered gunpowder brought up, but a lawyer protested: "Your Highness, it is against the rules of the Temple to blow up with gunpowder."

The Duke paid no attention. His Master of the Horse picked up a cudgel and hit the lawyer several times. Paper House was soon blown up, but flames continued to burn in the Temple. Finally, when the fires were almost out, the end of the roof of the Inner Temple Hall caught fire. Seaman Richard Rowe climbed up, and sitting astride the Hall's ridge beam, beat the flames out. Within a few minutes there was no more fire at the Temple.

Pepys had made arrangements for the royal dockyardmen that Sir William Penn had brought in to lodge in the Navy Office. At midnight, after he procured them drink, bread and cheese, Pepys went to bed on Will Hewer's quilt. When Pepys arose at five on Thursday morning, he was so bleary-eyed from lack of sleep he had trouble remembering what day of the week it was. It seemed incredible that only four days earlier the fire had started in Pudding Lane.

On his way from the Navy Office, Pepys met Dennis Gaudens rushing in. A merchant who supplied victuals to the Navy, Gaudens had come for the royal dockyardmen. Fire had broken out in Bishopsgate, the northeast area of London where up to now the fire had not reached!

The dockyardmen were soon ready with explosives and buckets, and with Pepys leading the way, they quickly marched into Bishopsgate and put out the flames. Afterward, Pepys sat down wearily and watched as neighborhood women swept up the excess water from the cobblestone streets. Butts of sugar were then brought up and opened. Everyone around scooped out handfuls of sugar

THE AFTERMATH

and poured them into beer. Soon men and women were staggering around the streets, getting "drunk as devils."

Although some areas would burn and smolder for days, the great fire of London was over. The air was calm now, and the huge conflagration that had leveled the City was a horrible nightmare. A detachment of two hundred soldiers marched in from an adjoining county to finish the mopping up. With carts piled high with spades, buckets, and pick-axes, they arrived at the fire posts and relieved the weary fire fighters stationed there. Later, more militia arrived from other counties.

London lay like the blackened crater of a volcano. For more than one mile along the Thames and a half mile inland, the City that only a week before had been a bustling metropolis of 600,000 inhabitants was now a broad expanse of smoking ruins, punctuated by gutted skeletons of churches and Company halls. Heaps of burned stone and rubbish lay everywhere, and heavy layers of black soot blanketed the entire area.

Strangely, the fire had taken little toll of life. The *London Gazette,* official government newspaper, claimed

later that no lives had been lost. The published Bills of
Mortality directly attributed only six deaths to the fire. Besides the Farynor maidservant and the man who dropped
dead near the Tower of London, the list included two
fatalities at St. Paul's: one an old woman overcome by
smoke, the other an old man who went into the cathedral to
retrieve a blanket and was suffocated.

The loss in property was a different matter. A survey
made later by the City revealed that five-sixths of London
within the ancient walls—373 acres in all—had been leveled.
Outside the City—in the Liberties—63 acres and 3 roods
had been burned. Flames had swept through more than
400 streets and lanes, and 13,200 houses had been destroyed, as well as 87 churches and 52 Company halls.

In the years that followed, attempts were made to
place a monetary evaluation on the loss. One early estimate
calculated the total loss to be 7,370,000 pounds. Another
made a century later estimated 10 million pounds. According to this calculation, the houses destroyed had a value of
3.9 million pounds, and St. Paul's Cathedral—2 million.
Another 2 million pounds was accounted for by the "wares,
household-stuff, monies and moveable goods" burned up.
While the "tobacco, sugar, plums, and warehouse stocks of
wine" destroyed were worth about 1.5 million pounds.

All in all, no one has ever challenged the statement of
the British historian Macaulay, who said: "A fire such as
[this] had not been known in Europe since the conflagration of Rome under Nero."

On Thursday, before the flames were completely out
at Bishopsgate, Charles II, accompanied by his gentlemen-
at-arms, left Whitehall Palace on horseback to survey the
burned-out City. Picking his way along the still smoking

streets, he found it difficult to concentrate on what needed
to be done. Food was scarce, and the water supply low.
Most housing had been destroyed, and few churches could
be used for worship. All markets except one had been
burned up, and the Post Office was put out of commission
as well as the Custom House. Huge inventories of coal,
timber, and naval stores had been lost. Business and commerce were wrecked, and the City had no place to hold
court or house its municipal offices. Even most of its prisons
had been demolished.

As Charles saw it, London had two immediate problems. One was to provide for the several hundred thousand
homeless camped outside the walls. The other was to restore as soon as possible London's government. Charles galloped to Moorfields and into the midst of his distraught
subjects. A crowd quickly gathered around him and a cheer
started, but he motioned for silence. Still mounted, with
London's walls at his back, and behind them the smoking
City, he looked into the sea of upturned faces. Speaking
rapidly but clearly, Charles explained the steps he had
taken to help the homeless, and then what he intended to
do further in this, the time of London's great trial.

Charles began by saying that he was immediately returning the government to City officials. He then said that
he had sent for Lord Monck to return from the fleet to help
maintain order in destroyed London. A professional soldier
who had served first under Charles's father, Charles I, and
then under Cromwell and the Parliamentarians, Monck
had been instrumental in arranging for Charles's restoration to the throne. During the Plague, when most of London was deserted, Monck had remained in charge of the
government.

KING CHARLES ADDRESSING THE CROWD

Charles also told the homeless about the food he had made available, and he said that he was also distributing to the poor twenty-five thousand pounds' worth of slightly burned but still usable wood. Then he turned to a subject he knew was in everyone's mind: the rumors that the Dutch, French, or Papists had started the fire. "I assure you," he said, "that this fire is immediate from the hand of God, and has resulted from no plan." Charles explained that he himself had examined many of those who had been detained as possible suspects, but he had found no evidence that indicated any plot. "There has been no connivance," he emphasized.

In concluding, the King urged everyone to be calm. "I have the strength to defend you from any enemy," he said. "And I assure you that I, your King, will, by the grace of God, live and die with you."

After Charles returned to Whitehall Palace, he issued an order restoring authority in London to Sir Thomas Bludworth; he also directed the Lord Mayor to assemble all aldermen, magistrates and "citizens of quality." Jointly with the King's Privy Council, this group would "care for the public welfare of the city."

The aldermen had already met that Thursday in Gresham House, the former mansion of Sir Thomas

Gresham which the merchant-banker had left to the City as a site for a college to bear his name. Its many rooms offered ample space for the municipal offices burned out at Guildhall. Also, in the quarters of Gresham College's professors, there were apartments in which the Lord Mayor, Sheriff, Town Clerk, City Chamberlain, and City Sword-bearer could live until they could rebuild their burned-out houses.

On Thursday afternoon, William Taswell, the student, started off on foot from Westminster to get a look at still burning St. Paul's. So heated was the air and so hot the ground that Taswell had to rest after a half mile to keep from fainting. When he reached St. Paul's, he noticed first its gutted walls, and then its huge Corinthian columns, blackened but still standing. The cathedral's heavy bell had melted, and Taswell picked up pieces as souvenirs. He had expected to stay longer, but as he watched, a tremendous stone that had become loose, crashed down—almost at his feet. Taswell returned immediately to Westminster.

Pepys also traveled to Westminster, but by boat. His clothes dirtied by the fire fighting at Bishopsgate, he hoped to purchase a new shirt and pair of gloves in Westminster, but its shops were closed, storekeepers having removed all their goods. After a stop at Whitehall Palace where he saw no one he knew, Pepys returned down the Thames. From the Temple past London Bridge, he did not see one house or church standing.

For the rest of the day Pepys kept going back and forth. He had his noon meal at the home of Sir Richard Ford, a hemp contractor. He went again to Deptford to check his goods stored there. He "supped well and mighty merry" at Sir William Batten's. He slept that night again at the Navy Office, which was now crowded with the Navy dockyardmen who "talked, slept, and walked all night long."

The next day, Friday, Pepys was up at five. He first blessed God because everything at last was well, and then once more he toured the stricken City. He saw "the miserable sight of Paul's church with all the roofs fallen and the body of the quire fallen into St. Fayth's." He also saw the ruins of St. Paul's School, which he had attended. Pepys borrowed a shirt from his cousin John Creed, secretary to the Earl of Sandwich. Then he walked over to St. James's Palace to exchange gossip with Sir William Coventry, the Duke of York's secretary. They chatted about the rumors sweeping London: that, despite what Charles had said, the Dutch or French had a hand in starting the fire, and that a movement was afoot to seek out the culprits and punish them. They also talked of how rentals for the houses still standing had doubled and tripled. A friend of Sir William Rider was asking one hundred and fifty pounds annual rent for a home that before the fire had rented for forty.

That same Friday, John Evelyn also toured the ruins. The going was tough. Evelyn had to climb over the still-smoking ruins, and when he misjudged where he stepped—which happened often—he burned the soles of his feet. Evelyn saw hundreds of other Londoners walking through the devastated City, wandering around "like men in some dismall desert." Smoke was still pouring from warehouses and cellars. Fountains were dried up; their waters had boiled away. In the streets, cobblestones lay piled up, and on some, heaps of melted silver plate and bell metal. The heat had even twisted door hinges and prison gates.

In his entire walk, Evelyn saw not "one load of timber

unconsumed, nor a stone not calcined." Except for a few blackened towers marking the site of a familiar church or company hall, Evelyn could not tell where he was. At Cheapside he could hardly believe his eyes. Because the fire had leveled all the buildings to the Thames, the view to the river—for the first time since Roman days—was unobstructed.

Another viewing London's ruins that Friday was Souchu De Rennefort, a captured French officer who had been released from military custody just one day before the fire. Curious to see what London looked like, De Rennefort procured a horse and galloped down Fleet Street from the Strand. At first he saw nothing amiss. Approaching the Temple, he found everything normal for a distance of about thirty houses. Then, after the thirtieth house—nothing. From that point on, not a single house was standing!

Friday night the thousands of homeless slept as before in the open fields, in makeshift accommodations or on the ground. Pepys was put up at Sir William Penn's. It was the first time in Pepys's life that he had slept in "a naked bed" without curtains or hangings. Even so, he slept well although not soundly. As Pepys wrote later in his diary, he had "a fear of the fire in my heart."

V

No man whatsoever shall presume to erect any house or building, great or small, but of brick or stone . . .

WITH NO MAIL out of London for almost a week, the rest of England heard only wild rumors about the great London fire. Panic spread quickly through the counties. Without logic or justification, magistrates arrested all the foreigners they could find, and incidents multiplied of attacks on Catholics, Anabaptists, and Nonconformists. At Barnstaple, the militia was called out in the belief that a plot existed to burn down all English cities. At Falmouth, the Governor detained the German ships in the harbor. At Norwich, still in the throes of the Plague, bellmen marched through the streets, calling out that no one should house strangers until the Mayor had examined them.

Already arrived in London, Lord Monck rode around the City Saturday morning, his presence helping to calm the troubled populace. But as Londoners started rousing from the effects of the terrible calamity, they began to seek explanations. That God's judgment had fallen on London, as Charles had said that day in Moorfields, most agreed. But whose God? The Catholics said that London's heresy and sinfulness had brought on divine wrath. The Quakers announced that London's destruction was the result of members of their faith being persecuted. Royalists considered the fire a retribution for the beheading of Charles I, the present King Charles's father.

Suddenly everyone remembered various prophets who had foretold the City's doom. Several decades before, a book entitled *Mother Shipton's Prophecies* had created considerable excitement in England. One of its prophecies told of a ship sailing up the Thames to London, its master weeping because no houses were left in the City where sailors could buy drink. When Prince Rupert, Charles's uncle who was at sea with the English fleet, heard the news about London's fire, he said: "Now Shipton's prophecy is out."

Less than a decade before, a pamphleteer named Walter Gostello had warned London to "Repent, or burn, as Sodom, as Gomorrah." In 1659, one Daniel Baker prophesied that "a consuming fire shall be kindled . . . which will consume with burning heat." The following year, a persecuted Quaker, Humphrey Smith, in his *Vision Which He Saw Concerning London,* described a fire that no one could quench: "All the tall buildings, and it consumed all the lofty things therein, and the fire searched out all the hidden places, and burned most of the street places."

A few months before, a veteran Parliamentary colonel had conspired to kill King Charles and Lord Monck. The plot had been discovered and all the conspirators executed. But now everyone remembered the date selected for the assassinations. It had been chosen for its astrological significance—the stars said it was auspicious for "the downfall of Monarchy"—and the date was September 3, 1666, just one day after the fire had started.

On Sunday, all Londoners who could crowd into the City's remaining churches attended services. Only twenty-two churches still stood (about one-fifth of those that had held services the previous week). Pepys attended his regular parish church, St. Olave's, Hart Street, but found most faces unfamiliar to him, and few of the strangers, he noted, were "of fashion." The minister, Nathaniel Hardy, delivered a melancholy sermon, and many in the audience, especially the women, cried.

That night, it rained in London for the first time in months. But fires still smoldered, and Charles warned that much combustible material remained. He urged the aldermen to order homeowners to remove debris from their property, and he also suggested that watches be established in every ward.

The next day, at Gresham House, the aldermen and also the Lord Mayor, sheriffs, and Common Council met. Arrangements were made to continue supplying the City with food, and to establish temporary markets. The ruins of Guildhall were directed to be cleared, and sheds to be set up in each ward where municipal officials could receive and give orders. Directions were also given to start clearing London Bridge that very night, so traffic to Southwark could be restored.

To aid those impoverished by the fire, the churchwardens of each parish were directed to furnish the Lord Mayor with a list of their poor. If they could, City Companies were to provide food, lodging, and other necessities to those of their members who needed them.

Within the next few days, the City began to awake. Shacks of beer-sellers sprang up among the ruins, and reappearing on the streets was the *London Gazette*. Its printing plant had been temporarily set up in a graveyard, and in its first post-fire edition on September 8, the single-sheet

Gazette published an official narrative of the great fire:

> The ordinary course of this paper having been inter-
> rupted by a sad and lamentable accident of fire
> hapned in the City of London [it started out], it hath
> been thought fit for satisfying the minds of His Majes-
> ties good subjects who must needs be concerned for
> the issue of so great an accident to give this short, but
> true accompt of it. On the second instant at one of the
> clock in the morning there hapned to break out a sad
> deplorable fire in Pudding Lane. . . .

Although most Londoners were still stupefied by the
destruction, some began to talk and think about rebuilding
the City. On Monday, September 10, Christopher Wren,
the recently appointed Deputy Surveyor of His Majesty's
Works, showed up at Whitehall Palace with a plan for a
new model city.

While parts of the City were still smoldering, Wren
had climbed over the ruins, working out the details. He saw
the fire, tragic as it was, as a great opportunity to rebuild
the City and to incorporate the best in municipal planning
that had been done in Europe, especially France.

Wren's model city called for opening up London so
that all its parts would be accessible, particularly London
Bridge. This Wren expected to accomplish by replanning
the City's streets. Gone forever would be the old London
with its narrow alleys and winding courts. Now crossing and crisscrossing the City would be boulevards, highways, and wide streets, many of which would terminate in
beautiful piazzas.

There were many unusual features in Wren's plan. The
old Fleet Ditch would be remodeled into a scenic and use-

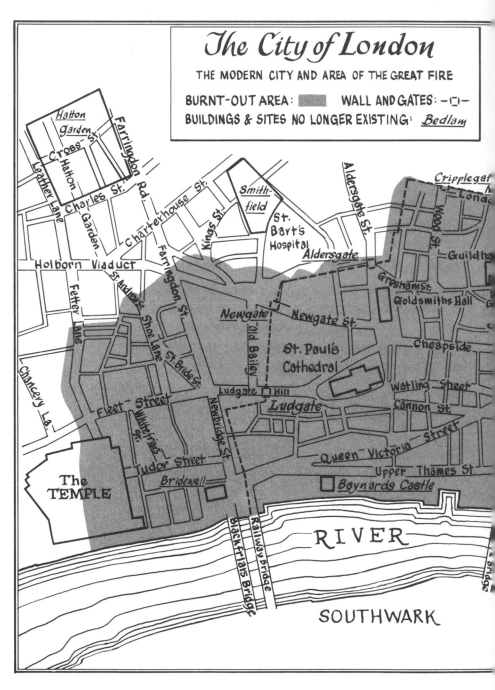

The City of London

THE MODERN CITY AND AREA OF THE GREAT FIRE

BURNT-OUT AREA: ▨ WALL AND GATES: –◻–
BUILDINGS & SITES NO LONGER EXISTING: *Bedlam*

Hatton Garden
Cross St.
Leather Lane
Hatton Garden
Charles St.
Farringdon Rd.
Charterhouse St.
Kings St.
Smithfield
St. Bart's Hospital
Aldersgate St.
Cripplegate
London
Wood St.
Guildhall
Aldersgate
Holborn Viaduct
Fetter Lane
St Andrew St.
Farringdon St.
Shoe Lane
Newgate
Old Bailey
Newgate St.
Gresham St.
Goldsmiths Hall
Cheapside
Chancery La.
St Bride St.
St. Paul's Cathedral
Watling Street
Fleet Street
Whitefriars St.
Newbridge St.
Ludgate Hill
Ludgate
Cannon St.
Tudor Street
Bridewell
Queen Victoria Street
Upper Thames St.
Baynards Castle
The TEMPLE
Blackfriars Bridge
Railway Bridge
RIVER
Bridge
SOUTHWARK

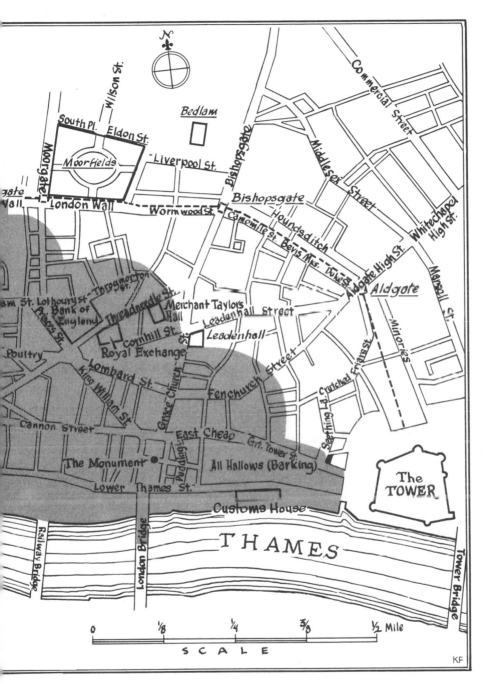

N

Wilson St.

Bedlam

South Pl. Eldon St.

Moorgate

Moorfields

Liverpool St.

Bishopsgate

Commercial Street

Middlesex Street

gate Wall

London Wall

Wormwood St.

Bishopsgate

Houndsditch

Camomile St. Bevis Mks. Dukes

Whitechapel High St.

am St. Lothbury St. Throgmorton St.

Bank of England

Threadneedle St.

Merchant Taylors Hall

Leadenhall Street

Aldgate High St.

Aldgate

Mansell St.

Prince's St.

Cornhill St.

Leadenhall

Minories

Poultry

Royal Exchange

Lombard St.

Grace Church

Fenchurch Street

Seething La.

Crutched Friars St.

King William St.

Cannon Street

East Cheap

Grt. Tower St.

The Monument

Pudding

All Hallows (Barking)

The TOWER

Lower Thames St.

Customs House

Railway Bridge

London Bridge

THAMES

Tower Bridge

0   ⅛   ¼   ⅜   ½ Mile

S C A L E

ful canal. The Thames would be lined not by docks and warehouses, but by a public quay that would stretch from the Temple to the Tower of London. The City's most important government buildings—the Excise Office, Post Office, and Mint—would be relocated on land plots around a new Royal Exchange, and also nearby would be an "Insurance Office."

The City churches would be relocated on main roads to make them more accessible, and they would not be surrounded by graveyards or gardens because these were "unnecessary vacuities." The "noisome trades" like soap boilers, breweries, and lime burners would be banished to areas designated by the Lord Mayor. To facilitate traffic, all houses would be removed from London Bridge. And in honor of Charles II, founder of the New London, Wren planned a triumphal arch at Ludgate.

Unknown to Wren, John Evelyn was also preparing a plan for a new city, and he presented it to Charles, the Queen, and the Duke of York the very next day. In many respects, Evelyn's plan was similar to Wren's. It too called for piazzas, a Thames quay, and the houses cleared from London Bridge. But Evelyn's street plan was simpler and his design more Continental. Evelyn advocated relocating the Royal Exchange to the Thames riverbank, and building on its former site an official residence for London's Lord Mayor. He also saw developing new areas. Around the new College of Physicians, for example, would be apothecary shops. Around St. Paul's would be an enlarged churchyard with a Bishop's Palace, a new house for the Dean, a new St. Paul's School, and—in a daring innovation —a public library.

Evelyn also saw churches surrounded by booksellers

and stationery shops. Church burial grounds would be outside the city walls, and opposite these grounds—also outside London—would be a street with taverns. As for Evelyn's Thames quay, it would have no projections or boat stairs. All warehouses would be moved to Southwark because they evoked "a dull and heavy experience," and they would be replaced on the quay with government buildings and homes of wealthy merchants.

The plans of both Wren and Evelyn were well received by Charles. As Evelyn wrote: "[He] examin'd each particular, and discours'd on it for neere an houre, seeming to be extreamly pleas'd with what I had so early thought on."

But Charles had a more urgent problem. Although hundreds of thousands of Londoners still camped outside London, many were returning to the City. Some returned to the ruins of their own houses, and as Lord Clarendon wrote, "with more Expedition than can be conceived, set up little Sheds of Brick and Timber." Others who had not owned homes previously burrowed into cellars of abandoned homes and built makeshift shelters. Then, on September 10, little more than a week after the fire had started, one enterprising citizen actually started rebuilding his house.

Charles immediately called a meeting of the Privy Council. Such action had to be stopped at once. If every Londoner began rebuilding his home when and if it suited his convenience, the new London would emerge a more haphazard city than the old one. London would end up probably uglier than before, and perhaps even more vulnerable to fire. No; Wren and Evelyn had the right idea even if their plans might turn out to be too impractical to implement. The fire had given Londoners an opportunity to rebuild a London more suited to contemporary needs, with fireproof materials that would prevent just such destruction as the old London had suffered.

Charles realized that he must act immediately to stop all unplanned construction. He must eliminate the confusion as to how the new London would be rebuilt. He must furnish the outline for rebuilding the City. He must do this quickly, without mistakes, and he must make sure in the efforts to achieve a new London that the rights of none—not tenant, nor landlord, nor businessman, nor church—were violated.

Regardless of the plan adopted, Charles had to come forward with concrete guidelines that would give direction to the rebuilding. Candles burned late in Whitehall Palace as the King, taking into account all the factors, drew up a general outline for the new London. On September 13, 1666, Charles made a historic royal proclamation.

He started off by describing London as more "convenient and noble for the advancement of trade than any other city in Europe." It was his desire that, with the help of its citizens, London *would* arise resplendent, "making it rather appear to the world as purged with fire (in how lamentable a manner soever) to a wonderful beauty and comeliness."

As set forth in Charles's proclamation, Cheapside, Cornhill, and "all other eminent and notorious streets" would be so wide that, "with God's blessing, [they] should prevent the mischief that one side might suffer if the other be on fire." No streets, particularly those near the river, would be so narrow that passage through them would be difficult. Unless absolutely necessary, the new London would have no alleys or lanes.

As Wren and Evelyn had suggested, London would have a Thames quay and a Fleet canal, and the noisome trades "which by smoke made adjacent localities unhealthy" would be relocated. To encourage the rebuilding of private homes, anyone who did rebuild would be exempt for seven years from the hearth tax, which every homeowner in England paid. And not one house in the new London would be constructed of wood. "No man whatsoever shall presume to erect any house or building, great or small, but of brick or stone," Charles proclaimed.

To facilitate rebuilding, Charles also called for a survey to be made to determine the ownership and dimensions of every land plot in London. Such a survey was needed, he explained, since no accurate street map of London existed. Once it was completed, no one could accidentally or deliberately build on property not his own; if he did, the Lord Mayor would have the right to tear the building down. The survey would also enable a model to be built of the City, showing how it would look rebuilt. In addition, it would give the City a basis for acquiring the footage necessary to widen streets, and it would also allow for land to be distributed if Wren's or Evelyn's plan was adopted.

In conclusion, the proclamation pointed out that sacrifices were expected of everyone, including the King, for the public good and for the future beauty of the City.

Charles had furnished the guidelines, but to translate his plan into an actual rebuilding program, specific legislation was needed from Parliament. Both Houses were summoned to meet in Westminster on September 18.

The King's first words to Parliament at the Westminster session were: "God be thanked for our meeting today. . . . Little time hath passed since we were almost in despair of having this place left to meet in."

Parliament immediately voted a resolution thanking Charles for his great efforts in fighting the fire; then a committee was appointed to consider the rebuilding. There were many days of debate but no legislation. Too many decisions remained unresolved. Should London be rebuilt completely, as Wren and Evelyn had proposed? Or should it be rebuilt on the old plan, with brick and stone houses being substituted for those formerly of wood? Or should the new London represent a compromise between the two approaches—rebuilt essentially as it was, except for streets being widened and a few new features added like the Thames quay and the Fleet canal?

Unable to decide, the Parliament committee turned its attention instead to the equally serious problem of financing the war with the Dutch. Charles could push Parliament no further. He himself—together with his Privy Council and London's officials—would have to make the decisions as to what type of new London would be rebuilt, and would have to draft the detailed legislative proposals so that Parliament could vote on them.

Meanwhile, other plans were submitted for a new London. The only one receiving serious attention came from Robert Hooke, England's most brilliant experimental philosopher. An extremely practical plan, Hooke's design called for key streets running east and west, bisected by other key streets running north and south.

Also submitting a plan was Captain Valentine Knight of His Majesty's Services. The chief feature of his plan was a thirty-foot-wide barge canal through London. As Knight explained it, the Crown could levy fees on the barges, and Charles could expect to receive at least two hundred thousand pounds in income annually. Charles's reaction was to jail the officer. How could anyone even suggest that he would consider profiting from a public calamity of his people!

Slowly, business and commerce were beginning to revive. Within a week after the fire, the first shops were reopened by the ruined Royal Exchange on a pavement constructed from stones and bricks brought over from the ruins around Guildhall. Shortly after, merchants began conducting business at Gresham House. By October, Guildhall was completely cleared of debris, and the following month, a temporary wooden building was erected there to hold court sessions.

Although the fire was now an event of the past, alarms were still frequent—flames kept shooting up in different areas of the City despite the fact that most combustible material had been cleared away and fire watches set up in each ward. Some warehouses near St. Paul's had been burned out weeks before, or so it had been thought; but workmen sent there found that the goods inside blazed up as soon as they opened the warehouse doors.

Crime now became a problem in London. As thousands of Londoners moved back into the City, thieves and plunderers—as Lord Clarendon described them, "ready enough to fish"—came with them. From outlying towns bad characters journeyed to London, ostensibly to seek work in the rebuilding, but actually to steal from the homeless. A royal proclamation commanded all persons who willfully or ignorantly appropriated property not their own to bring it within eight days to the Armory at Finsbury Fields. But no one showed up.

Several weeks later the Lord Mayor issued a proclamation calling for the punishment of "vagrants, beggars, and loose and idle persons" caught wandering in the ruins. To discourage thefts further, aldermen put up stocks and whipping posts in each ward, but apprehension of looters proved difficult. Most constables and watchmen were still homeless and had not yet returned to their duties.

Other English counties and cities were sympathetic to London's plight. Lyme Regis in Dorsetshire collected one hundred pounds and dispatched it to London for the aid of the distressed. Lynn in Norfolk delivered food in a convoy escorted by a warship. Private citizens also contributed. A group of clergymen, for example, handed over almost seventy pounds to the Bishop of London.

From Ireland, Lord Ormond wrote Sir Thomas Bludworth, offering cattle to the stricken city; money was in too short supply. To accept the cattle, an Act of Parliament forbidding the importation of Irish cattle would have to be amended. London made many requests for the amendment, but Parliament ignored it.

To broaden the appeal and increase the funds, Charles proclaimed a day of fasting and humiliation throughout all England and Wales. Its purpose was "to implore the mercies of God, that it would please him to pardon the crying sins of this nation, those especially which have drawn down this last and heavy judgement upon us." On the date selected—October 10—not only were special services to be held in all churches, but also collections for the needy of London.

When the day arrived, Dr. Sancroft, Dean of St. Paul's,

preached a two-hour sermon before Charles and the Court at Whitehall Palace. Pepys with Sir William Batten tried to attend St. Margaret's, but it was too crowded. So the two went to Dog Tavern and ate herrings instead, attending another church in the afternoon.

When the collections from England and Wales were counted, they totaled a disappointing 12,794 pounds. Some cities never made collections; others that did never forwarded them to London. Of the money received, Devonshire sent in the largest amount—almost 1,500 pounds. The smallest donation—four pounds—came from the ward of Cheap.

Despite Charles's insistence at Moorfields that no plot was involved in the great fire, many Londoners were not convinced. Recognizing that bitterness against foreigners and Papists would increase, Charles sent for Sir John Kelyng, the Lord Chief Justice, to head a Privy Council investigation that would settle once for all the question of whether any individual or group had been responsible for starting the fire.

For weeks, Kelyng and the Privy Council examined all those arrested during the fire on the grounds of possible conspiracy. Testimony was also heard from witnesses reporting suspicious incidents. Hundreds eventually testified. Women had seen mysterious strangers hurl into houses various objects that burst into flames as soon as the strangers were out of sight. Men told of odd-looking individuals who threw on burning houses "water" that intensified the flames, rather than quenching them.

Little Edward Taylor, the ten-year-old son of an

apothecary, took the stand. He said he had been walking with his uncle and father the night the fire broke out. When they had reached Pudding Lane, the two men tossed fireballs into the open window of a house. His uncle, the boy said, gave his father seven pounds to throw the fireballs.

Such testimony was suspect, and so, most believed, was the testimony of Robert Hubert, a French watchmaker seized in Essex after the fire, apparently trying to flee the country. A man with the reputation of having a disordered mind, Hubert confessed. Yes, he had started the great London fire. It was part of a fantastic plot. The year before, when he had been in Paris, plans had been made for him and accomplices to burn down London. They had arrived in London on a ship from Sweden and had been taken into the City the night of the fire. At Pudding Lane, Hubert said, he put a fireball at the end of a pole and stuck it through a window, keeping it there until the house caught fire. All this he did, Hubert said, for the reward of a pistol.

Hubert's story had many discrepancies. Even Farynor, who insisted that someone had fired his house, admitted that Hubert's description of it was inaccurate. Yet, when Hubert was taken by jailers on a tour of London, he pointed out in the ruins exactly where Farynor's burnt-out house stood. A court found Hubert guilty, and he was hanged. But, in spite of his confession, few, including the judge who sentenced him, believed Hubert guilty. Later it was discovered that the Swedish ship which had brought Hubert to England had not arrived until two days after the fire had started.

VI

The design of building the city do go on apace . . .

WHILE CHARLES SET about the enormous task of making basic decisions about the course of the rebuilding, London's municipal government began restoring disrupted functions. Meeting at Gresham House, the Common Council appointed different committees for different tasks. One surveyed municipal buildings to see which ones could be repaired for temporary use. Another met "to advise and consider" rebuilding Guildhall. Another concerned itself with refitting the compters and other prisons.

The royal government offices were also starting to function again. An improvised Custom House was established in Lord Bayning's house, the Excise Office was relocated in Southampton Fields, and a provisional Post Office was set up in Bishopsgate. Markets, too, were reestablished. Besides the ones that Charles had ordered set up the day after the fire, new markets were installed at Leadenhall for meat, fish, and leather, and at Aldersgate for herbs and roots.

Few Londoners were able to forget the fire. Pepys still slept uneasily, dreaming of flames and collapsing buildings. Many buildings still smoldered, despite torrential rains that had fallen for ten consecutive days in October. Two months later, Pepys, walking to Old Swan Tavern, saw a cellar burning, and soon after that, while driving by coach to Whitehall Palace, he observed "many smokes of fire . . . yet."

These smoldering fires added to the death toll. In October, one Richard Yrde was suffocated in a still burning house, and several weeks later the poet Shirley and his wife died—both on the same day. The exertion of fleeing London and sleeping on the ground had proved fatal.

Suspicion of a foreign plot never died. Now not only was Sir John Kelyng making an investigation; so was a committee of Parliament. At one of its hearings, Sir Richard Browne dramatically produced two hundred "desperate daggers fit for massacres." He said he found them in the rubbish of a London house where, before the fire, two Frenchmen had lived. Mrs. Elizabeth Styles repeated a conversation she had had six months before with Sir Vere Fan's French servant. "You English maids will like Frenchmen better when there is not a house left between Temple Bar and London Bridge," he supposedly said. "This will come to pass between June and October."

The hearings never seemed to run out of witnesses. A doctor in Old Bailey said he saw a stranger throw combustible material into an apothecary shop. A Southwark brewer said he found a fireball hidden in the shop of a wheelmaker. Even Belland, the King's fireworks maker, came under suspicion. When some pasteboards he ordered did not arrive on time, he had reputedly told the stationer, "I must have them by Tuesday [two days after the fire started], for after that I have no occasion for them." When asked what the rush was, Belland supposedly became embarrassed and talked instead of the fireworks he was planning for the next royal show. One, he said, would be a pure body of flame higher than St. Paul's.

Belland eventually proved his innocence, and no real evidence of a plot ever turned up. But a severe reaction took place against England's Catholics. Parliament forced Charles to agree to a series of restrictive anti-Papist laws. All priests and Jesuits were ordered to leave England by December 10. Anyone refusing the oaths of allegiance to England's Protestant government was to be disarmed. Not even Parliament was immune from these restrictions. The House of Commons voted that all members would receive the Protestant Communion. Any who abstained would be arrested.

But uppermost in everyone's mind was the rebuilding. Initial excitement over the plans advanced by Wren, Evelyn, and Hooke faded. From an architectural point of view, all of them left much to be desired. All three called for the obliteration of many familiar landmarks and streets, and Evelyn's plan had recommended considerable construction in stone, a very expensive building material compared to brick. Wren's plan preserved not one of London's historic highways and made no provision for growth. Too, his Thames quay would have severely reduced London's valuable shipping trade, since vessels could no longer load and unload directly at riverfront docks and warehouses.

Another major disadvantage of the plans was that they would take too much time to implement. To purchase all the land necessary for new streets and government sites would require years of legal proceedings. What would happen meanwhile to the hundreds of thousands of Londoners living in open fields outside the walls or in temporary habitations inside the City? Obviously, many would migrate to other English towns or to the colonies. What too would happen during all those years of legal bargaining to England's economy which rested squarely on the trade of

London, the nation's largest city and chief port? Not only that, but London was the largest single contributor of tax revenues to the Exchequer, and unlike other counties and cities, it paid its taxes on time.

An even more serious drawback to the plans was their cost. Vast sums of money were needed to pay for the land for the new streets and buildings, and neither the City nor the national government could raise the required funds. London's municipal government was impoverished. For years it had spent each year almost twice as much as it received in revenues. These deficits were made up by borrowing from merchant-bankers on a short-term basis (long-term loans were unknown then), and also borrowing from orphans' funds left in its custody. But so much had been borrowed that there were no more reserves to draw on; a few weeks after the fire, the City informed Charles it had no possible means of raising the estimated one hundred thousand pounds needed for the restoration of its municipal buildings.

London was so poverty-stricken that after the fire it even had to dispense with the usual pageantry accompanying the traditional swearing-in ceremony for the new Lord Mayor. The City could afford only a few marshals in livery, and the grieved Pepys wrote in his diary: "But Lord! to see how meanly they now look, who upon this day used to be little Lords, is a sad sight, . . . and everybody did reflect with pity upon the poor city."

With the City unable to finance its own rebuilding, everyone turned to the national government, but its financial position was hardly any better.

Charles had inherited a bankrupt Exchequer, with debts remaining from Cromwell's days and some even

Pepys keeping his Diary

from his father's. Each year the tax revenues that Parliament voted Charles were insufficient to pay his expenses, and more often than not, the monies voted were never received in entirety, since tax collections invariably fell short of estimates. Adding to the national government's financial predicament was the war with the Dutch. The Exchequer never had enough cash, and government officials like Pepys were continually being badgered by contractors demanding payment of bills, or employees seeking their wages.

Because of the fire, the national government would have even less income. Every house in England was taxed with a hearth tax. With 13,200 homes destroyed, receipts would be lowered considerably. Also, because of the warehouses and docks destroyed, customs revenues would be reduced, and even the proceeds from excise taxes would now be less.

Despite this dire situation, a few thought that Parliament, which alone had the power to levy taxes, could somehow try to raise funds to finance the rebuilding, and some proposals were actually made. One member suggested a special national rebuilding tax. Another proposed that sums be advanced to London to be paid back later from future tax receipts. Still another put forward a startlingly modern proposal. The national government would purchase all the land in the City, put it in trust, and then sell house plots, giving priority to those who had owned the land previously.

But in face of the nation's poor economic position and the war with the Dutch, all these proposals came to naught, along with any chance to adopt Wren's, Evelyn's, or Hooke's plan for a new model city. As a result, Charles and London had no choice but to concentrate on rebuilding a better city on the old foundations, and immediate steps were taken to complete the street and house-plot survey which Charles had proposed in his rebuilding proclamation. Orders were issued: London homeowners would have to survey their property; all those who owned or occupied land were directed to make "a perfect Survey of the ground whereon his House, Shop or Warehouse stood, with their Appurtenances, and his Right and Term therein."

Unfortunately, rubble—in some areas, four feet high—covered London, and no one could survey his property until this rubble was removed. Most homeowners were not up to the task, and laborers to do the clearing were almost unavailable. Individual surveys only trickled into the booths set up in each ward to record the information.

To facilitate the surveying, Charles recommended that contractors be called in and hired to do the surveying for a fee of one shilling for each land plot. Arrangements were so made, and to supervise the contractors, Charles appointed three Royal Rebuilding Commissioners, one of whom was Christopher Wren. The City appointed three official City surveyors to act as its supervisors. They included Robert Hooke.

But no sooner did the Rebuilding Commissioners and the City Surveyors meet with the contractors than problems developed. The contractors now wanted a higher fee, and they refused to survey any land plot unless someone else cleared it.

Two more directives were issued, urging homeowners to clear their land and explaining that all those who did would win the approval of the King, while those who did not would "undergoe such punishment and penaltyes as are due to their refractoriness, over and above his Majesty's displeasure."

By November, 1666, when it began getting cold and the survey was still hardly underway, Charles and the City recognized that further delay was serious. The government could not undertake the expense of clearing the land; to do so would give official approval to those who had disregarded the clearing directives. But perhaps if a start could be made at surveying the streets, this would encourage homeowners to clear their land. Charles himself donated 100 pounds to remove the rubble from the streets, and the merchant-banker Backwell loaned the city 200 pounds to pay for the street-staking.

Momentarily, the mood of London brightened. Pepys, after a conversation with one of the Rebuilding Commissioners, reported that "the design of building the City do go on apace, and by his description it will be mighty handsome."

But many Londoners wondered if rebuilding were progressing rapidly enough. One Parliament member wrote that "if things were not speedily provided for the merchants and wealthiest of citizens [they would] remove themselves and their estates into other counties, and so the City would remain miserable for ever."

The surveying of the streets failed to produce any increase in clearing or surveying houses, and although a workable street map finally was drawn up, the accurate map of land plots that Charles had envisioned had to be abandoned. Even so, out of the incomplete survey came one inadvertent repercussion that gave the rebuilding its biggest boost since Charles's proclamation.

With little to do while the arguments with the contractors continued and the surveying languished, the Rebuilding Commissioners and City Surveyors turned their attention to the detailed rebuilding provisions needed for the legislation to be submitted to Parliament.

Week after week, in the bitter cold of winter, the group met—often with Charles joining the sessions—in Whitehall Palace and Gresham College. Specific questions were asked, with the answers adding up to a master plan that would see London not only rebuilt, but "reborn greater and fairer than ever."

Should London's streets be located exactly as before? What widths should they be? What about rainspouts and garbage gutters? What about houses? Should there be a building code for houses? How many stories should London's new houses have? Of what materials should they be constructed? How could the City best supervise this construction, and what powers should it have to enforce this supervision?

The answers to these and hundreds more questions were spelled out in a series of Rebuilding Bills which, step by step, provided for the construction of a new London over the ruins of the old City. Every improvement that Charles had outlined in his original rebuilding proclamation was included. The streets of the new London would be wide enough to permit easy passage of all traffic. There would be four different types: "Key" or "High" streets 100 feet wide; "Other" streets either 50 feet or 42 feet wide; "Minor" streets 30 feet or 15 feet wide, and "Alleys"—if there had to be any—16 feet wide.

For the first time the streets of London would have uniform footages; no jutties or bows would be permitted. No rainspouts would splash water in the faces of passersby, since spouts now would be affixed to the sides of houses, and the spouts would carry the rainwater directly into the gutters. London, also for the first time, would be able to supervise street-paving, and to tax for it. And—another first —it could appoint sewer commissioners and levy sewer taxes.

As for house construction, only brick or stone could be used—no wood exteriors would be allowed. Jerry-built houses were also banned, so the new London would no longer have cheap tenements for the poor. In the new city, only three types of houses would be permitted, each of

OFFICIALS DISCUSSING NEW STREET PLANS

which would have to conform to standards both of building materials and dimensions. Houses fronting "high and principal streets" would be four stories tall. Houses on "streets and lanes of note and the Thames" would be three stories high. All other houses would have two stories. Ceilings would be either ten feet or nine feet high, and cellar depths, garret heights, wall thicknesses, and scantling sizes would also be of specified dimensions. To ensure that building regulations would be met, the City would be empowered to hire inspectors who would visit building sites and fine anyone not rebuilding according to the regulations.

As Charles had set down in his original proclamation, "dangerous and offensive trades" would be removed from the high streets in the new London. Also, legislation was provided for anticipated problems. To ensure that homes and other buildings would be rebuilt properly, standards were set for materials such as brick, tile, and lumber. To make sure these materials would be available at reasonable prices, the bills gave the City the power to reduce prices if suppliers charged too much. An adequate supply of labor to do the rebuilding was also ensured. Revoked was the right of craft guilds to prohibit all but their own members from working in London. Carpenters, joiners, bricklayers, plasterers, and other artificers from other English counties would be invited to London, and for seven years they could work unrestricted at their trades in the City.

One clause in the Rebuilding Bills was aimed at discouraging Londoners from moving to the suburbs. A veritable exodus had taken place for years, men working and trading in London relocating their homes in areas just beyond the City's jurisdiction. By doing so, they avoided responsibilities which were formidable. If elected to municipal office, a London citizen had to pay a four hundred-pound fine or accept the office. If he chose to accept, he often found himself working almost full-time at a responsible, nonsalaried job, like supervising tax collections or holding inquiries.

Now the Rebuilding Act made it impossible for a suburbanite to avoid municipal responsibilities. Anyone living within twenty miles of the City walls was a Londoner by law.

The Rebuilding Bills also provided the financial means for London to restore its damaged public buildings. The one hundred thousand pounds needed was to be raised by taxing coal entering the port of London. Since coal was already taxed, this tax would be additional surcharge, the revenues to be used solely for rebuilding. Taxing coal had many advantages. The collection machinery was already set up. The tax burden would be shared by all England, since coal entered London for many other counties and cities. Because coal was imported in large quantities, adequate revenues could be anticipated. Such a tax did not discriminate, since everyone used coal. Evading a coal tax was impossible: No coal substitute existed then, and coal's bulk made it almost impossible to smuggle.

Of all the Rebuilding Bills, the one most revolutionary —and at the same time most important—was a special bill providing for the settling of lawsuits and disputes between landlords and tenants of the burned-out houses. Incredible as it may seem, most leases had required tenants to keep the premises in good repair: If a house burned down, the tenant was legally liable, in most instances, to rebuild it. Despite the law, no tenant could think seriously of rebuilding if he would be bankrupted in the process, particularly when the subject of the lease—the house—was no longer in existence.

Complicating this situation was the fact that the exact ownership of a particular house was not clear cut. Land and property in London was divided among thousands of freeholders, leaseholders, subtenants, and quitrent owners. The arrangements by which these different groups participated in ownership were complex, and on them rested London's entire economic system. Since houses and land were the only safe investments, all marriage dowries, pensions for the aged, and estates of minors were tied up in property. The funds of every church, from huge St. Paul's to the smallest parish church, were invested in real estate. Universities like Oxford and Cambridge, hospitals, charity funds that dispensed food and coal to the poor in winter— they all depended on house rental fees for their income. Even the City of London derived one-quarter of its income from real estate, and Charles also depended on his fee-farm rents in London for revenue.

The fire had so scrambled everyone's rights that settlement by normal legal procedures was impossible; this would prove an unsurmountable obstacle to the rebuilding. Thus, the special Rebuilding Bill was designed to "prevent troubles and contentions betwixt Landlords and Tenants of Houses destroyed in the late dreadfull fire."

The chief feature of this unusual bill was the establishment of a special Court of Fire Judges, which would hear all cases involving landlords, tenants, and others unable to agree on an equitable settlement of any controversy resulting from burned-out property. What made the Fire Court unique was that it could take testimony, examine witnesses, and hear cases without any of the usual legal formalities. Also, the Fire Court had unusual powers. It could cancel existing leases and substitute others in their places, and it could even order new leases. The only appeals permitted were to a larger Court of Fire Judges, and all decisions here were final; no other court in England could reverse its judgment.

On November 30, 1666, the Rebuilding Bills—after having been passed by the Common Council—were sent to Parliament for approval. But Parliament, still occupied with the resolution of the financial problems of the war with the Dutch, did not act quickly. Charles used all the pressure he could, and only his awareness of London's urgent need kept him from ending the session. When Parliament did agree to debate the bills, opposition developed, and Charles in mid-December had to send a special message urging Parliament to press on with its considerations for new taxes and all bills outstanding. He warned there would be no adjournment until all business was concluded, and said if Parliament did not act, he would limit its Christmas recess to chief festival days only.

By December 31, 1666, the bills still had not passed, and Londoners began to get discouraged. "The City [is] less and less likely to be built again," Pepys wrote. "Everybody settling elsewhere, nobody encouraged to trade." Every time Parliament began to consider the bills, it was sidetracked. By the end of January, Charles dispatched another note, stressing the urgent need to settle London's affairs.

Somehow this brought the desired response. Suspending all other business, Parliament began debate on the Rebuilding Bills. Joined into one general bill, they passed their third reading in the House of Commons on February 5, 1667. The House of Lords made a few amendments but caused no delay. Three days later, Charles gave his royal assent. The "Act for the Rebuilding [of] the City of London" was now a law.

VII

Now began a little to revive
after its sad calamitie . . .

AFTER THE NEW YEAR, 1667, London suffered one of the worst winters on record. The Thames froze over, and in February, the City experienced the coldest day that anyone in England could ever remember. Huddled in lean-tos and in cellars, Londoners somehow endured, and with the passage of the Rebuilding Act, everyone's spirits rose. Pepys spent an entire evening studying its provisions. "I pray to God that I may live to see it [London] built in this manner," he wrote in his diary.

But still, many details needed to be worked out. On the last day of February, Thomas Hollier, a surgeon, grumbled to Pepys. He wanted to start rebuilding his house, but so many regulations were unclarified in the Rebuilding Act, he felt "unsafe to begin."

The starting point in the rebuilding was to classify the streets. The Rebuilding Act had specified the types and dimensions of streets in the new London, but it did not specify which streets would be which types. The City's Common Council undertook the task of street classification. Day after day in the bitter-cold winter, its members met at Gresham House, and with a large map of London before them, they went over every street in the new London, classifying it and determining its width and degree of straightness.

REBUILDING

When the map was finished, it was taken to Charles. With his finger, the King traced out the streets of the new city as the Common Council had determined them. In most cases, Charles agreed with the decisions made, but sometimes he suggested reclassifications. Lombard Street, he said, should be wider. The wealthy goldsmith-bankers who would rebuild there could easily afford the four-story houses called for by a "High" street classification. Charles also suggested that market stalls no longer be allowed to be erected right in the streets, blocking traffic as they had done for years at Leadenhall, Newgate, and Cheapside. Instead, market stalls in the new London should be built in market areas removed from main thoroughfares where they would not obstruct street traffic and would be easier to regulate and keep clean.

By the end of April, 1667, the street plan was completed and approved. As soon as the ground thawed, surveyors began the street-staking, the first street staked out being one near ruined St. Paul's. In the staking, one or two owners lost sizable strips of land to a new, widened street, but most had to part only with a narrow width. Then, in May, the first house-plots were staked.

The procedure was set by law. Whoever was rebuilding—homeowner or tenant—first engaged a builder. When the builder was ready to build, he went to Gresham House and entered in the record his name and the site. After paying a surveying fee of six shillings eightpence, the builder was given a receipt, and once he showed this to the City Surveyor responsible for the district, the two walked over to the building site, which had been cleared earlier. Usually the homeowner or tenant was there, and—if there was a dispute about boundaries—the owners of the adjoining properties. The City Surveyor listened to all allegations and then made his decision. If he allowed the staking to proceed, he "set out" the foundation, taking dimensions and measuring the walls and piers as specified in the Rebuilding Act. Then the workmen appeared—carpenters, masons, bricklayers, and other artificers—and the rebuilding began.

In the next few months here and there over London, staking took place amid the acres of blackened debris, gutted walls, and windowless, roofless churches. Day after day, the sound of hammering was heard as carts rumbled into the ruins bringing bricks, tile, lumber, and other materials to building sites.

The Rebuilding Act, with its provisions for guaranteeing an adequate supply of building materials at reasonable prices, worked well. The clause which gave the City the power to lower the cost of any material whose price was considered excessive, never had to be enforced, although bricks at one point became "somewhat dear" in cost. Bricks had never been needed in such quantities before, but the brick trade had no trouble meeting the demand. Many wealthy men like John Evelyn invested in new brick kilns, and private citizens in Moorfields and St. Giles-in-the-Fields were encouraged to look for land containing brick clay and to "digg and cast upp [this] ground." So enthusiastic were some diggers that they broke into buried water pipe.

Timber used for interior construction was also in adequate supply. The well-organized timber trade was accustomed to meet heavy demands on short notice. That winter, merchants had gone into the countryside, buying up lumber in anticipation of the rebuilding. Pepys and Sir William Penn invested in a company formed to ship wooden boards in from Scotland. Later, when lumber supplies got tighter, England relaxed the Navigation Act so that timber could be imported from Norway. So much lumber was eventually imported that it was said the Norwegians warmed themselves comfortably by the London fire.

Because the Rebuilding Act had standardized the types of homes in the new London, supply was facilitated and construction time shortened. Standardization also reduced the possibility of bad workmanship. With guild restrictions lifted by the Act, workmen migrated to London from all sections of England. A joiner from Dublin, a carpenter from Surrey, a painter from Oxford—all came to London, where wages were higher than in their own counties. Also streaming into the City seeking work were ex-soldiers as well as master and apprentice craftsmen uprooted by the Plague. In their case, as in the case of building materials, the Rebuilding Act provision against overcharging never had to be enforced. The wages demanded by guild craftsmen were high, but not excessive.

The most controversial section of the Rebuilding Act —the Court of Fire Judges—could not have functioned better. Twenty-two judges were assigned to this court, and little more than two weeks after the Act was passed, the Fire Court handed down its first decisions. As the judges saw their responsibility, it was twofold: First, to determine not who was legally responsible to rebuild, but who could rebuild quickly; second, to amend previous leases in such a way that rebuilders would be encouraged and the other parties involved would receive equitable compensation.

If, for example, a landlord could pay for the rebuilding—and his tenant could still afford to live there—the Fire Court would break the old lease and draw up a new one giving the landlord higher rent. If, on the other hand, the tenant was broken in fortune and had no prospects for resuming his trade, the Fire Court could cancel his lease and require him to pay the landlord only a token sum to get out of it. If the landlord was impoverished and the tenant could pay for the rebuilding, the Court could reduce the tenant's rent and give him a longer lease to encourage him to rebuild. And if neither the landlord nor tenant could afford to rebuild, then the Fire Court could order the Lord Mayor to seize the site and resell it to someone who could rebuild, with the rebuilder compensating the former owner.

The Fire Court was one of the most revolutionary legal concepts in English law since, in effect, it negated all previous law. Clauses, indentures, covenants, and forfeitures that had been in force for centuries—these the Fire Court had the power to cancel. Such a power was necessary to avoid legal entanglements that would delay the rebuilding by taking years to unravel. As the Act itself explained the Fire Court:

> Many of the Tennants, undertennants, or late occupiers whereof are lyeable unto Suits and Actions to compell them to repaire and rebuild the same, and to pay their Rents, as if the same had not been burned, and are not relievable in any ordinary course of Law, and great Differences are like to arise concerning the said Repaires, and new Building of said Houses, and payment of Rents, which if they should not be deter-

mined with all speede, and without change, would much obstruct the rebuilding of the said Citty; And for that it is just, that everyone concerned should beare a proportional share of the losse, according to their severall Interests . . .

The legal procedure used in the Fire Court was extraordinary. All testimony had to be given without lawyers, and no legal maneuvers were permitted to delay proceedings. Decisions were usually handed down the same day—sometimes within hours. All told, some seventy decisions were made by the Fire Court during the first year's sessions. Only a few appeals were made, and in each case, the original decision was upheld.

Sarah Andrews, a widow, owned a house on Fenchurch Street which she rented to William Phillips, an apothecary. The lease, for twenty-one years, called for an annual rental of 40 pounds. But when the house was destroyed in the fire, Phillips—even though the lease called for it—refused to rebuild. He also refused to pay rent on the destroyed house. Into this stalemated situation the Fire Court moved. Estimating the rebuilding cost to be 400 pounds, it ordered Mrs. Andrews to rebuild, and it directed Phillips to pay one-third the cost. When rebuilding started, he was to pay 33 pounds. When the first story was raised, he would owe 50 more, and when the house was completed, he would owe another fifty. Rebuilding started several weeks after the Fire Court handed down its decision.

The Thames River water system case was more complicated. Built almost a century before by Peter Morris, the system had been highly profitable, and Morris left it to his heirs. Before the Restoration, finding management by many to be difficult, the heirs turned over the system's

THE FIRE COURT

operation to a group of trustees headed by Thomas Morris. He was to pay them annually from "the Rente and profitte," but when the fire destroyed the system, Morris stopped payments—and also did not begin rebuilding. Again the Fire Court moved to activate the situation. Deciding that no equitable agreement could be reached until the repair cost was known, the Court had an estimate made. Two thousand pounds was the calculation, and the Court found a third party willing to undertake the rebuilding at that cost under the condition that he would be paid from the initial profits of the rebuilt system. The Fire Court then created three new trustees to operate the system and resume annual payments to the heirs. Thomas Morris, temporarily ousted by this decision, was to be returned to control after twenty-one years. Morris was agreeable to the arrangement, as were the heirs, new trustees, and rebuilder. Rebuilding started soon afterward. The Fire Court had not only worked out an equitable arrangement among all parties; it had, more importantly, restored a vital link in London's water supply.

A few diehards were able to circumvent the Fire Court's authority. Humphrey Henchman, Bishop of London, was landlord for many booksellers and mercers on Paternoster Row who were willing to rebuild, but wanted their rents reduced if they did so. Henchman refused their offers, saying he would do nothing until they paid their back rents—even for the time after the fire when the houses were no longer in existence. When a stalemate developed, the mercers and booksellers tried to take their cases to the Fire Court, but Henchman, also a member of Parliament, claimed the right to be immune from any Fire Court decisions. As a result, the mercers and booksellers could proceed no further.

Another area in which the Fire Court had no jurisdiction was where homeowners wished to protest the footage taken from their properties to widen streets. Here the City of London had to resolve disputes. One William Wheatley petitioned the Common Council to reduce the land seized from him. Seven feet wide and sixty yards long, the strip, Wheatley argued, could just as easily be taken from the *other* side of the street.

Wheatley was turned down, but John Saunders was more successful. Living on Fetter Lane, he petitioned to have the width of the entire street reduced, and the City approved the change. Similarly, inhabitants of Huggen Lane protested that if their street were made fourteen feet wide, as the new regulations specified, it would become a regular cart route and its paving would be broken up and its doorways made unsafe. They asked for the "improvement" to be rescinded, and the City granted their request.

The controversy between John Hammond and Anthony Selby started out as a minor land dispute and ended up in Parliament. Both wealthy men, they owned adjacent property on Mincing Lane, one of the streets to be widened. When several feet of frontage were taken from both men's property, Hammond accepted the loss and started to rebuild along the new boundary lines, but Selby tried to get the staking altered. When he failed, he simply removed the stakes and reset them on Hammond's property. When Hammond protested, the City found that the frontage of an entire row of houses being built on Mincing Lane by Selby projected illegally into the street, in some places as much as five feet. Ordered to correct this condition, Selby instead protested to the Privy Council, and when it refused to consider his case, he appealed to the House of Commons, which appointed an investigating committee. The City retaliated by obtaining court orders forcing Selby to move back the houses. When Selby refused, the City purchased the houses, rebuilt them properly, and rented them out at a profit.

All the funds to pay for the rebuilding of London's houses came directly—or indirectly, through loans—from private citizens. Since no savings banks existed then, all money and jewelry were stored in iron chests similar to the one that Pepys carried to Woolwich during the fire. When Pepys's cousin, Anthony Joyce, asked for a loan to rebuild his house, Pepys was quite "willing to have some money out of my hands on good security." He simply opened his chest —which contained 2,350 pounds in gold—and handed over to Joyce the gold he needed.

Similarly, although Nelly Denton had no money to

rebuild her home, her family did, and they lent her the necessary funds. Nicholas Barbon, the economist and entrepreneur, also had no trouble borrowing money at 6 percent to rebuild the Lock and Key Tavern in Fleet Street.

Helping to loosen the hold on available personal funds were ministers like Samuel Rolle. Sunday after Sunday, Rolle in his sermons urged the wealthy to lend all the money they could to prospective rebuilders. Such lending had not only spiritual values, he claimed, but was also the most profitable investment a Londoner could make. Certainly, Rolle pointed out, it was better than the 6 percent maximum to be earned in foreign-trade investments.

Some Londoners had been so ruined financially by the fire they could not rebuild themselves nor could they borrow for rebuilding. Everything owned by Lady Gardiner had been burned up, including "all my sone had to depend on and my girls." Widow Sarah Crofts was reduced overnight to poverty, and she and her daughters were forced to become servants. Thomas Catchmead, a wealthy fishmonger, lost his entire fortune of 7,000 pounds in the fire and had to appeal to Charles for permission to open a small fish stall in the Strand.

Because of the financial losses of private individuals, the King—harassed by debts before the fire—found himself more besieged than ever by petitioners seeking money he owed them. Elizabeth Proctor, widow of Charles's deceased vintner, petitioned for 600 pounds due for wine which had been furnished the King four years previously for the entertainment of the Prussian Ambassador. The King's current vintner, Sir William Hale, also demanded what he was owed. During the fire he had lost his house and entire wine stock. James Gamble, one of the King's musicians, had not been paid his salary in five years. Because of the fire he had been unable to pay his debts, and he told Charles that he faced debtor's prison if his salary was not forthcoming.

New houses slowly began to rise in London. By December, 1667—about fifteen months after the fire—some 650 of the 13,200 houses destroyed had been rebuilt, and by the spring of 1668 the total reached 800 houses. Still, everywhere one looked in London, there was rubble. The few new houses standing on some streets seemed swallowed up by the ruins. Even optimists like Reverend Samuel Rolle were discouraged. "Methinks it is an ill prospect, and a ghastly sight," he wrote, "for these that look from balconies, or tops of their stately new houses, to see ashes and ruinous heaps on every side of them." So sparsely built was Cheapside that merchants did not move back immediately into their newly built houses. Until the neighborhood became more populated, they feared that trade would be too unprofitable, and chances of being robbed too great.

But by the summer of 1668, rebuilding picked up. More than twelve hundred houses now stood, and one thousand more were under scaffolding. So many workmen had moved to London by now that labor shortages existed in the counties outside London. Because of the migration of skilled workers to London, the Royal Dockyard at Sheerness had to close down temporarily. By the end of 1669—about three years after the fire—several thousand houses had been rebuilt, and sixteen hundred more were under scaffolding.

In September, 1669—on the third anniversary of the fire—John Evelyn took a walk around London, just as he had done in 1666, when the ground was still hot. He spent "almost the intire day in surveying what progress was made in rebuilding the ruinous citty." And he noted that it "now began a little to revive after its sad calamitie."

By this time the City of London had made considerable progress in restoring its damaged public buildings. Borrowing from private individuals against anticipated revenues from the coal tax, it had rebuilt most of the compters and jails, and repaired all the boat stairs. Its biggest single project—the rebuilding of Guildhall—had been launched the year following the fire. The architect was Christopher Wren, and his plan called for the new Guildhall to be built on the foundations of and within the still standing walls of the previous building. Wren proposed raising the height of the historic building twenty feet, and constructing a new roof and gallery. His proposal also included constructing many surrounding buildings such as a Town Clerks' Office, Common Council Chamber, and Mayor's Court Room.

By the summer of 1667, the scaffolding had been erected at Guildhall, and London's morale received a boost. Six months later, construction had proceeded so well that Pepys noted it in his diary, and by May, 1669, Guildhall's exterior was completed.

Rebuilding had also started on several important government buildings in London. Construction had begun on the Custom House by 1667. Wren again was the architect, and the site was that of the destroyed Custom House.

Another major project was the rebuilding of the Royal Exchange. Edward Jerman, one of the City Surveyors, was the architect here, and in April, 1667, before the site was cleared, Jerman toured England looking for suitable stone.

By September he had his designs ready, and the following month, accompanied by kettle drums and trumpets, Charles galloped into London with the Duke of York and Prince Rupert to lay the first pillar. After the ceremony the royal visitors were entertained in a shed erected over the ruins, and Charles gave the workmen 20 pounds in gold.

But construction of the Royal Exchange did not proceed smoothly. Owners of adjoining land needed for the new building refused to sell, claiming they intended to build on the property themselves. When Jerman got a court order forcing them to sell, their answer was to set an impossible price. In desperation, Jerman then proposed to reduce the Royal Exchange's size, but he died before he could draw up new plans. Thomas Cartwright, the contracting mason, took over as "master of the wholle design intended," and he followed through on Jerman's revised plans. By the end of 1669, construction had moved ahead so well that merchants were able to return to the inner quadrangle.

The City Companies began rebuilding their Halls far less rapidly. Their problems were almost insurmountable. More than fifty Halls had been destroyed; only seven had survived the flames. The Companies had also suffered extreme financial losses, losing not only their valuable silver plate but also their endowment funds, which were almost exclusively tied up in houses. Some Companies never did recover from the great fire. Others that did rebuild accumulated the necessary funds only with difficulty. The Merchant Taylors obtained rebuilding funds by salvaging from the ruins of their Hall the silver plate and lead from the roof that had melted, and also from selling valuable property. The Barber Surgeons Company raised 1,250 pounds

REBUILDING THE MERCHANTS TAYLORS HALL

by soliciting subscriptions from its members. The Plumbers Company was able to borrow money from Sergeant Peter Brent, the King's Plumber. Such efforts paid off. By the end of 1669—three years after the fire—more than a half-dozen Company Halls were in the process of being rebuilt.

Meanwhile, Companies kept up their activities the best they could. Some untouched by the flames invited burned-out Companies to hold meetings in their Halls. Carpenters Hall, which was still intact, extended its hospitality to the Goldsmiths, Drapers, Weavers, and Feltmakers Companies.

The rebuilding of the churches did not start until years after the fire. Eighty-seven churches had been destroyed, and the Rebuilding Act called for thirty-nine to be rebuilt. Delaying construction was the fact that the Rebuilding Act did not specify which thirty-nine. Every time the matter was considered, controversy resulted—so much so that authorities avoided further problems by ignoring church rebuilding and concentrating their efforts on other rebuilding.

The work of the churches continued, even though most church buildings consisted of only four blackened walls. A few churches (like St. Michael's, Wood Street) were able to be patched up, but mostly, services had to be held elsewhere. Some churches (like St. Mildred-in-the-Poultry) accepted the offers of City Companies which made their Halls available. Others set up their parish headquarters in rented rooms. Then, in August, 1669, the parishioners of Allhallows the More started a trend when they erected a shed or tabernacle on the ruins of their original church. Many other churches followed suit, paying for the construction of these tabernacles by selling their melted bell metal and roof lead. Some also constructed pews in the abandoned churchyards and doors in burned church walls.

Although parishioners had the right to be buried in their own parish churches, burial often became difficult when the sites of the churchyards could not easily be determined in the ruins. At St. Bride's, one Christoper Riche was buried "in ye church porche, because ye body of ye church was not cleere." Ann Yard was placed to rest in "the burring place where before the lat dreedfull fire the lat church of St. Pancras Soper Lane stood."

St. Paul's was the exception to the lack of activity in church rebuilding. A religious symbol to all England, the great cathedral was in everyone's mind after the fire. A few weeks after the King's proclamation, Wren spent several days surveying the ruins to assess the damage and see if the cathedral could somehow be restored rather than rebuilt. Analyzing its structure almost stone by stone, Wren prepared for Charles a detailed report which concluded that, although the cathedral could conceivably be patched up,

Wren was sure the King would not like the result. "What Time and Weather had left entire in the old, and Art in the new repair'd parts of the great Pile of S. Pauls, the late Calamities of the Fire hath so weakened and defac'd that it now appeares like some Antique Ruine of 2000 years continuance," Wren wrote. "To repaire it sufficiently will be like the mending of the Argo-navis, scarce anything will at last be left of the old."

What Wren recommended was the construction of a new St. Paul's, his reasoning being that "a more durable and notable Fabrick" would have to be constructed sooner or later. However, Charles rejected this advice and ordered Wren to repair the giant building and to build by the following summer a temporary chapel in the safest remaining part of the cathedral: "between the West End and the second Pillars about the little North and South Doores."

The first task Wren had was to clear out the rubbish, and this was soon accomplished, 47,000 cartloads being removed eventually from the site. Then the damaged columns had to be pulled down. Here Wren recommended using gunpowder, but the City vetoed the idea on the grounds that the noise would frighten everyone. Wren got the temporary chapel completed in time, and in September, 1667—on the first anniversary of the fire—Dean Sancroft, St. Paul's Dean, delivered a special sermon. Charles himself was in attendance.

But six months later, just as Wren had predicted, the temporary chapel collapsed. Wren, at Oxford, received an urgent letter from Dean Sancroft. A big stone had fallen from the wall, damaging the vaulting, and the following day, one of the huge pillars had collapsed, carrying the scaffolding and everything else nearby to the ground. "The

Second Pillar (which you know is bigger than the rest),"
he wrote, "stands now alone, with an enormous weight on
the Topp of it; which we cannot hope should stand long,
and yet dare not venture to take it down."

The Dean begged Wren to return as soon as possible
to London with those "excellent Draughts and Designs you
formerly favour'd us with," and also to consider what advice he should give regarding the cathedral to the King and
all England. Wren had dreamed for years of how he would
redesign St. Paul's if he ever received the opportunity. Just
before the fire, when he had inspected the cathedral with
Evelyn and others, Wren had visualized St. Paul's not as
the huge Gothic cathedral it was, but as a graceful Renaissance cathedral resembling those he had seen on the Continent. In making his recommendations then, Wren had
suggested that the cathedral's previously destroyed spire
should not be rebuilt, but rather be replaced with a "spacious Dome or Rotundo with a Cupola."

Answering Dean Sancroft, Wren said that in his opin-
ion the only worth of the destroyed St. Paul's was its possible use as a "quarry" to supply stones for a new cathedral.
He assumed, he said, that lack of funds would prevent the
erection of "any more such huge Piles," and he said he was
in favor of some "neate Fabrick which shall recompense in
Art and Beauty what it wants in bulke."

Dean Sancroft replied that Wren was mistaken. England wanted a cathedral as noble and handsome as possible
—one that would represent the greatness of London and
the nation. Whatever the expense, money would be found
to build it. All that was needed was an accepted design. He
implored Wren to "prepare something to be propos'd to his
Majesty" and asked him to start with the choir as part of

"a greater and more magnificent work to follow."

Wren did work up new designs, and after returning to London to show them to Charles, the decision was finally made to rebuild—not to repair. The King made it official in July, 1668, by issuing a Royal Warrant authorizing the rebuilding.

For months after the fire, London was not safe at night. Robbers and murderers stalked the streets, and the constables and watch were unable to offer full protection to the citizens. In a 1667 letter, Postmaster Hickes complained of Londoners being carried into cellars, victims of robbers posing as linkboys. "No person dare, after the close of evening," Hickes wrote, "pass the streets amongst the ruines." A year after the fire, Pepys, returning home after a play, became frightened when he learned that thieves had broken out of Newgate Prison. Later, walking through a ruined churchyard, he became fearful again when he was approached by two ruffians with clubs, but again he was not harmed. Even so, as Pepys wrote in his diary, he was tired of taking the safe route home every night—walking around outside the City walls in order to escape the dangers within.

In the summer of 1667, London faced a far worse danger than robbers and murderers, namely, an attack by the Dutch. For months England had not been active in its war against Holland. The combined demands of the war, the Plague, and the fire had drained England's resources. The nation was in such dire financial straits that the fleet could not be reequipped after the winter drydocking, and the Navy could not meet its payrolls. The previous January some unpaid sailors had started a riot in the Strand, and it was quelled only when Charles himself rode in to talk to them.

The Dutch were also anxious to end the war, and when feelers were sent out, a peace conference was arranged at Breda, Holland, to take place several months later. In the meantime, the British laid up their fleet and assumed the Dutch had done the same. But Admiral De Ruyter had a bold plan to force more favorable peace terms for the Dutch. He decided to sail his fleet to England and attack shipping in the port of London.

On June 6, 1667, the Dutch fleet suddenly appeared off the English coast, and twenty Dutch men-of-war began moving up the Thames. English shore batteries raked the invading ships, but at the crucial moment, they ran out of shot. Moving on, the Dutch ships broke through a chain stretched across the Thames, and then passing ammunitionless English gunships anchored in the river, they drew near the Tower of London.

Drums sounded in the City, summoning everyone to arms. Charles already had hurriedly called out the militia and troops, and they had begun assembling on the riverbanks. Fireboats were sent out against the Dutch ships, but to no avail. Lord Monck a few hours before had sunk frigates and merchantmen in the river to serve as a blockade, but the Dutch ships crashed right through.

Then, while the thousands of citizens and troops lining the banks looked on with horror—unable even to fire because of the enemy's superior firepower—the Dutch men-of-war trained their cannon on the English Navy ships and merchantmen in the port. Hundreds were sunk in the next few hours, including three first-class Navy warships. The *Royal Charles,* pride of the English fleet, was made fast to a Dutch ship and towed down the Thames.

THE DUTCH FLEET
CAPTURED THE 'ROYAL CHARLES'

With mainsails billowing, the Dutch ships soon sailed away down the Thames, disappearing into the North Sea, carrying the *Royal Charles* to Holland, and to the rest of the world the news of England's humiliating defeat.

No sooner had the immediate danger passed than London panicked. Rumors flew that Charles had fled and the government had dispersed. But Charles rallied the nation as he had done during the great fire. Calm followed, but when the peace treaty was signed later at Breda, the English agreed to amend the Navigation Act which called for all imports to be brought into the country in English ships manned by English sailors. This meant that Dutch ships could trade directly with England. At this time, also, the English exchanged Surinam in the East Indies for the Dutch colony of New Amsterdam in North America. In honor of Charles's brother, the Duke of York, it was promptly renamed New York.

The Dutch humiliation of the English only intensified the agitation in London against foreigners, and again resentment flared up against those who were suspected of "firing" the city during the great fire. Still, no evidence had ever turned up that any plot existed. The Parliamentary committee investigating the fire drew no conclusions when it issued its report. It simply compiled the testimony of hundreds of witnesses. One member of the House interpreted this testimony to signify that the "Fire was of wicked design," but Parliament pursued the investigation no further.

Similarly, the investigation by the Privy Council revealed no evidence of a plot. "Nothing yet hath been found to argue it to have been other than the hand of God upon us, a great wind, and the season so dry," its report concluded.

Extremists refused to accept these verdicts, and not able to pinpoint blame for the fire on foreigners, they channeled their hatred toward Catholics. Even the Royal family was not spared in their attacks, particularly the Duke of York, whose sympathies toward Catholics (Charles's and the Duke's mother was a Catholic) were well known. The Duke's heroism in fighting the fire was ignored. Now all that extremists could remember was that he "looked too gay" during the fire.

In 1669, as every year since the fire—and indeed every year for almost two centuries after—a special service was held in September commemorating the event. Yet Londoners needed no ceremony to remind them of the great fire. The memory of it had never left the hearts and minds of those who had lived through the four terrible days. New fires breaking out occasionally in the ruins or among the rebuilt houses would cause a fleeting panic—until it was realized that Londoners never again would experience a similar disaster. Relieved, they would then look around their city and also realize that more—much more—needed to be done to complete the rebuilding of London.

VIII

London rises again . . .

BY 1670, WILD FLOWERS still grew in uncleared London lots, and hundreds of Londoners still lived in temporary habitations, but the rebuilding of the City's houses was nearing completion, and unbroken rows of neat brick houses lined many streets. Many town houses had also been constructed, and in Old Jewry, Sir Robert Clayton opened the doors of his elegant mansion in which London's future Lord Mayors would give many splendid entertainments and banquets.

Construction had also been progressing well on government and municipal buildings. The Custom House was completed at a cost of 10,000 pounds by the end of 1670. A new King's Beam had been erected, and three new markets—at Stocks, Newgate, and Honey Lane—were in the process of being built.

The chances were that when a vacant lot did exist now, it marked the site of an abandoned or unbuilt church. These church sites were London's single biggest eyesore. On some, tabernacles had been erected, but most were still full of rubble. At night, thieves made their headquarters in these uncleared churchyards, and during the day they were often taken over by blacksmiths and storekeepers who set up their businesses there. In other abandoned churchyards, housewives hung their wash, the clothes fluttering over the graves.

The reasons for the delay in rebuilding the churches

were many. As Londoners were told repeatedly, not all rebuilding in the new city could be carried out simultaneously, so the churches had had to wait until most of the houses and public buildings were rebuilt. But besides this, the decision had never been made as to which of London's churches would be rebuilt. The Rebuilding Act had called for thirty-nine churches to take the place of the eighty-seven destroyed. This meant that more than half the old parishes would have to be combined. The Bishop of London and the Archbishop of Canterbury had been appointed to draw up the list, but every time they announced their decisions, parishioners of absorbed churches protested and threatened to take legal action. As a result, the list of the thirty-nine churches to be rebuilt was still not finalized.

Still another reason for the delay in church rebuilding was that no money was available to pay for it. Church construction was to be financed—as was also construction of public buildings—by the coal tax. As the Rebuilding Act had established this tax, it was to provide the 100,000 pounds the City estimated it would need to rebuild the churches and public buildings. But in three years, only 23,000 pounds had been collected, and one year—1667— had seen receipts of only 800 pounds.

The City's answer was to sponsor an Additional Rebuilding Act, which was expected to produce extra revenues for church rebuilding and also to fill in a few loopholes and omissions in the original act. Passed by Parliament in 1670, the Additional Rebuilding Act increased the coal tax from one shilling per ton to three shillings per ton. Three-fourths of the two-shilling increase was earmarked solely for rebuilding the churches; one-fourth of the increase was to go directly toward rebuilding St. Paul's.

Because of the pressure, the Bishop of London and the Archbishop of Canterbury had agreed to increase the number of churches to be rebuilt from thirty-nine to fifty-one, and in the Additional Rebuilding Act, the specific churches were enumerated. Considerable combining still had to take place; under the new arrangement, the rector of St. Margaret's, Lothbury, was rector of seven other parishes besides his own. But the list was set legally now, and construction could start.

Before the end of 1670, rebuilding had started on fourteen churches, and architect for all of them—indeed, for all fifty-one—was, incredibly, one man, Christopher Wren. Indefatigable, Wren had already rebuilt the Custom House and was in the process of rebuilding Guildhall. He was now Surveyor-General of His Majesty's Works (advanced from the deputy position when his predecessor died), and also a Rebuilding Commissioner. And, above all, he was the principal architect of St. Paul's.

Characteristically, Wren threw himself into the church-rebuilding too. In some churches, notably St. Christopher-le-Stocks and St. Mary's, Aldermanbury, he was able to use existing walls and simply recase them in stone. In others, like St. Mary-le-Bow, St. Olave Jewry, and St. Michael's, Cornhill, he could rebuild on the original foundations. But for most churches, Wren had to demolish what structures remained and rebuild completely.

The Additional Rebuilding Act had also provided legislation for two unique projects that Wren had originally proposed, and that Charles included later in his historic proclamation: the Fleet canal and the Thames quay.

Wren had visualized transforming the Fleet Ditch into a forty-foot-wide barge canal. The Rebuilding Act had

paved the way for this canal by authorizing the City to
purchase the land and to prohibit the construction of unde-
sirable structures near it. The Additional Rebuilding Act
spelled out the details. The canal would be navigable at
least a half mile up from the Thames to Holborn Bridge.
Wharves would line both sides, and under them would be
underground storehouses. Back of the wharves—fronting
the canal on both sides—would be uniform lines of neat
brick houses.

Construction of the Fleet canal began in 1670, the
year the Additional Rebuilding Act passed. First, the lines
of the channel and wharves were staked out in the presence
of the royal surveyors. Then, contracts were let to build
experimental hundred-foot sections of the canal. A contractor named Thomas Fitch was awarded the contract to
build the canal and, to do the job, he had to overcome tremendous obstacles. During construction, mud and refuse
kept choking the river, and rubbish piled up on the wharves
he was leveling. Also, unknown springs caved in excava-
tions periodically, and water from a nearby creek kept
flooding the uncompleted channel. But Fitch persevered.
Keeping two hundred full-time men on the site, he completed the task of carrying away the dirt in baskets, and
then he constructed the channels and wharves. In 1674,
when the Fleet canal was opened, Fitch received a gift of
plate, and, later, a knighthood.

Construction of the Thames quay proceeded more
slowly. To provide for the land, the Additional Rebuilding
Act had banned all sheds, fences, and buildings from the
riverbank. But houses had already been built along the
Thames from the Tower of London to London Bridge.
Since their builders had followed regulations, these houses

made a good appearance and had straight fronts, giving
the riverfront the appearance of a quay—even though one
had not been built.

As a result, the City allowed these houses to stand and
concentrated on the section of the riverfront from the
Bridge to the Temple. First, the line of the quay and the
position of the boat stairs and docks would be demarcated.
Then, after eight months, the ground would be leveled.
After that, construction would begin.

Everything went according to schedule, but when the
lines were staked out, the City got another idea. The dirt
being dug up in constructing the Fleet canal could be used
to straighten the front of the Thames quay. London then
would have one broad, straight quay, eighty feet wide,
along the river. Wren was enthusiastic, and so was Charles.
Construction of the quay along these new lines began.

Business and commerce had almost completely re-
vived in the new London. So many carts and drays rattled
into the City each day that a policeman—London's first—
had to be hired to direct the traffic at London Bridge. By
November, 1671, Guildhall was so near completion that it
was used for the elaborate ceremony of the Lord Mayor's
Feast. The Royal Exchange was almost finished also; merchants had been conducting business there for several
years. Many Company Halls like those of the Vintners
Company and Parish Clerks Company had also been completed, and several others, like the Tallow Chandlers, were
halfway through construction.

Then England suffered a severe economic reverse.
Adding to the strain of the Plague, fire, and war on the
nation's finances, the cost of rebuilding London had di-
verted capital that should have been used to build up Eng-

land's foreign trade. The government had trouble meeting its financial commitments. The royal dockyard workers, who had not been paid, mutinied.

Charles had long sought new sources of revenue, and in 1670, financially harassed, he had let himself be persuaded by Louis XIV of France, his uncle, to sign the secret treaty of Dover. Charles would receive 150,000 pounds a year, in return for which he was to announce his conversion to Catholicism and to join Louis XIV in a land-sea war against the Dutch.

Louis XIV paid the subsidy, but not until 1672 did he ask Charles for military and naval assistance in the war against the Dutch. Anxious to avoid fighting both on land and sea, the Dutch gave no opening for the English to start hostilities, and finally, to precipitate the war, some English warships had to be ordered to attack a Dutch convoy returning from Smyrna in the English Channel.

ENGLISH FLEET ATTACKS DUTCH

This started the war, but soon afterward the English fleet, commanded by the Duke of York and the Earl of Sandwich, Pepys's cousin, was surprised by the Dutch Admiral De Ruyter. In the resulting naval battle which the English lost, Sandwich's flagship was burned and Sandwich was drowned.

Unlike the other two Dutch wars, this one was unpopular. Charles, criticized on all sides, did not fulfill the other provision of the Treaty of Dover—the announcement of his conversion—but he did issue the Declaration of Indulgence, which offered freedom of worship to Catholics in their own homes and to nonconforming Protestants in their places of worship. The populace reacted unfavorably. Dissension spread further when suddenly the Duke of York declared publicly that *he* had become a Catholic.

The unrest that followed in London created a problem that no one would have thought possible a few years before: many of the rebuilt houses had no tenants. Entire rows were deserted along certain streets, and as one Londoner wrote, "no person so much as asks the price of any." A survey hurriedly conducted by the City revealed that 3,423 of London's new houses were unoccupied.

Actually, only 9,000 new homes had been rebuilt, the difference between the 13,200 destroyed being the elimination of many substandard homes as well as the fact that an estimated 25 percent of London's pre-fire population had left, never to return. Only about 450,000 inhabitants of the original 600,000 still lived in the city. So serious was this loss in population that a Dr. Denton complained, "the depopulation is soe vast it cannot afford us a livelihood."

Where had all the "missing" people gone? No one

knew exactly. Some merchants, it was known, had moved
to Liverpool and set up companies to trade with the Ameri-
can colonies. Other families had migrated to St. Helena
under the auspices of the East India Company. But most,
it was thought, had simply moved to other cities or counties, not being able to afford to wait until the City was
rebuilt.

The City decided to try to get back everyone it could.
All aldermen were ordered to return with their families,
and all City Companies were told that their members must
live in the City. To encourage shopkeepers to move to London, the City enacted laws similar to those in the original
Rebuilding Act that had brought workmen and artificers
to London from other parts of England. Then, by law, the
guild restrictions that had prevented "foreign" carpenters,
bricklayers, and other craftsmen from working in London,
were set aside. Now these same types of restrictive regulations were nullified for shopkeepers like grocers, mercers,
and stationers who were also so badly needed.

The strategy worked. Even though many former London shopkeepers had become settled in new locations, the
attractions of being in business again in London proved
powerful. Also, shopkeepers who had never lived in London moved there. A button-maker from Gloucester, an
apothecary from Oxford, a trader in Indian gowns from
the Strand—slowly London's unoccupied houses became
tenanted.

In 1673, Charles knighted Christopher Wren, who was
working harder than ever in rebuilding the City. Five years
later, the first fourteen churches were completed, and
Wren had already begun construction on six more, including St. Mary-le-Bow. Despite the fact that Wren was the

architect for all the churches, he managed to impart to each an individual architectural distinction. With St. Stephen Walbrook, it was the dome. With St. Bride's, the beautiful Renaissance steeple. With St. Mary-le-Bow, the tower. For St. Laurence Jewry, Wren designed a magnificent vestry with a carved fireplace; for St. Michael's, Cornhill, a striking Gothic tower. Only one of the fifty-one churches rebuilt had the same architecture as before—St. Mary's, Aldermanbury. A parishioner donated 5,000 pounds to rebuild it on the condition that nothing would be changed.

In 1673 Wren was also able to return to his beloved St. Paul's—the one major rebuilding task remaining and the biggest single project in the entire rebuilding program. Very little had been done on the great cathedral since the decision had been made years before to rebuild it. Other rebuilding projects had siphoned off most available workmen and materials. But now, with practically all of London's houses, company halls, and public buildings rebuilt— and church construction well underway—attention could be turned to St. Paul's.

When Charles had originally issued his warrant to authorize rebuilding the cathedral, it had been thought that some of the existing foundation and walls could be salvaged, but Wren, in the intervening years, had convinced Charles that these had no value and should be removed. As a result, a supplementary warrant was issued in 1673, stating that "It is now become absolutely necessary totally to demolish and raze to the ground all the relicks of the former Buildings."

Massive and strong, the blackened walls of St. Paul's were two hundred feet high in some places, and Wren this time received permission to pull them down with gun-

RAZING OLD ST. PAUL'S

powder. He himself supervised the operation. Holes approximately four feet square were dug in the supports and masonry, and into them, canisters containing about eighteen pounds of gunpowder were placed. The explosions were heard for miles around, and to many who felt the shock, they seemed like earthquakes.

Later, Wren had to abandon gunpowder. Once, when he was out of the City, a subordinate used too much powder, and a wall fragment flew across the site and crashed into the window of a nearby house. Londoners petitioned the King to have the walls pulled down another way; and Wren came up with a novel idea, an adaptation of an "ancient Engine of War"—the battering ram. Constructing a huge ram that took thirty men to operate, he had it positioned in front of the wall to be torn down, and then drawn back and allowed to hit hard, again and again, against the wall.

The first day the ram was used, the wall remained standing after hours of battering. When workmen told Wren the ram was a failure, he insisted they continue; no wall could stand such a battering much longer. The men resumed battering, and the wall eventually fell with a crash, its debris carted away to be used as street-paving material.

Once all the walls were down, Wren began the more difficult task of removing St. Paul's old foundations. When this was completed several months later, Wren dug test holes for the cathedral's new foundation. His diggers brought up everything from bones of sacrificed animals to Roman pottery. The new St. Paul's would rise on a spot that had been used for religious rites in Britain since the earliest times.

Wren then had a scaffolding erected from which he could plan the design of the new cathedral. Standing on this platform day after day, he kept sighting positions, and one day he called to a workman to bring him a stone so he could mark his position. The workman picked one out of the rubble. A fragment of a tombstone, it had one word chiseled on it—*Resurgam*, meaning, "I shall rise again."

As yet, no design had been approved for the new St. Paul's, despite the fact that Wren had submitted several through the years. One which featured a Renaissance dome and a floor plan in the shape of a Greek cross, had been turned down by the clergy, who said they preferred a tower instead and a floor plan shaped like a Roman cross. It was said that Wren wept when this design was rejected.

Another Wren design showed two domes, and a

lengthening of the cathedral's east and west lines. Charles gave his approval, and even commanded Wren to make a wooden model "thereof to be made after so large and exact a manner that it may remain as a perpetual unchangeable Rule and Direction for the conduct of the whole work." But this design was eventually rejected too, and Wren was so embittered that he left London, saying that he had been put into a position of trying to please too many "authorities," and that such a situation did "but lose Time and subjected his Business many times to incompetent judges."

When Wren finally did return, he began a new set of designs in which he incorporated just about *all* the major suggestions made to him. St. Paul's now would have a Renaissance dome, but on top of that would be a tall spire similar to the one that had once topped the ruined cathedral. Much to Wren's surprise, this design was accepted by everyone. Charles gave his approval in another Warrant, and more important, he added a clause giving Wren the power to alter any features as he saw fit during the construction. On June 21, 1675, Wren's master mason laid the cornerstone; construction—which would take more than three decades—began shortly afterward.

Almost a decade had passed since the great fire of London. Pepys was still secretary to the Navy Board, but many changes had occurred in his life. His wife Elizabeth had died suddenly of fever during a European vacation. The Navy Office and the Pepyses' home on Seething Lane which had survived the great fire, burned down in 1672. Because of trouble with his eyes, Pepys had stopped writing his diary.

Then Pepys inadvertently became involved in anti-Catholic agitation. Parliament had forced Charles to cancel his Declaration of Indulgence which gave Catholics the right to worship freely. It also pushed through the Test Act, which banned Catholics from holding government office. Even the Duke of York was affected by the new law. Forced to choose between his new Catholic religion and his position as Lord High Admiral, he resigned from the Navy, and Samuel Pepys—to administer the Navy—was elevated by Charles to the new position of Secretary of the Affairs of the Admiralty of England. As such, Pepys had more authority over England's naval forces than any civilian before or since his time.

England simmered down, and commerce and trade picked up in 1674, when, after several inconclusive naval engagements, the English pulled out of the war with the Dutch. But four years later, the country was rent by another political crisis. A renegade Jesuit novice named Titus Oates and a Protestant clergyman, Israel Tonge, claimed to have discovered papers revealing a vast Jesuit conspiracy to assassinate the King, put the Duke of York on the throne, and impose Catholicism by sword over all England.

As weeks passed, Oates and Tonge fed more sensational details to the increasingly excited populace. The Queen, a Portuguese Catholic, was involved in the conspiracy, they said; she was to have poisoned the King. Also, London was to have been fired—and by the very same Jesuit conspirators whom, Oates and Tonge claimed, had fired the City in 1666 and had never been apprehended.

England's temper rose, particularly when Sir Edmund Berry Godfrey, the Protestant magistrate who first heard Oates's charges, was found mysteriously murdered, run through by his own rapier. Catholics were jailed en masse, and investigations launched. Titus Oates was revealed to be a perjurer, and the letters to be forgeries. But bitterness against Catholics only intensified. Pepys, because of his long association with the Duke of York, was accused of having Catholic leanings and betraying naval secrets. Forced to resign his secretaryship, he was committed to the Tower of London, and although charges were eventually dropped, he lost his Navy position.

Again the intense political feeling abated, and by 1683, London was bustling once more. Very little rebuilding remained. Twenty-five churches had now been rebuilt, seventeen were nearing construction, and only on six had rebuilding not started. Wren had made tremendous progress at St. Paul's, and by this time had surrounded himself with a team of artisans that became well known in their own right for their artistic contributions to the cathedral.

On this team were Tijou, the great French ironworker; Francis Bird and Gabriel Cibber, stonecarvers; and Philip Wood, woodcarver. Wren's most famous artificer was Grinling Gibbons, his chief woodcarver. (John Evelyn had discovered Gibbons. Walking home one day to Sayes Court, Deptford, he happened to look into the window of a thatched hut and saw a young man—Gibbons—carving in wood a re-creation of Tintoretto's painting depicting the crucifixion of Christ. Having seen the original in Venice, Evelyn was astounded at Gibbons's artistry and took him to Whitehall, where he presented him to Charles, and later to Wren.)

Tons and tons of building materials went into the construction of St. Paul's, and the quantity of stone used was tremendous. All types from marble to chalk were required, but most stone was Portland stone, which came from the royal quarries at Portland, a small island in the English

BUILDING THE
NEW ST. PAUL'S

Channel off Dorchester. Permission had to be granted from
Charles to procure this stone, and special roads and piers
had to be built to work it. To transport the Portland stone
to London, a regular fleet of ships had to be assembled.
Lighterage charges alone came to almost 29,000 pounds.
In all, it cost about a half-million pounds to rebuild St.
Paul's. Approximately one-fourth the cost went toward
purchasing the stone.

Although London had almost completely recovered

from the fire, life for Charles had not become less hectic. His economic problems had never improved, the nation's religious differences seemed irreconcilable, and foreign intrigue forced him to continue to plot and scheme with Europe's monarchs. Yet, as he continued to serve as England's King, Charles also maintained his active personal life. He still took long walks, although not so many as in younger years. He worked in his science laboratory, attended races at Newmarket, and celebrated the Queen's birthday by arranging lavish fireworks displays on the Thames.

As the years passed, and Charles became plagued with gout and ague, he began to think more and more about his successor. Since he had sired no legitimate children, his most probable successors were his brother, the Duke of York, and his oldest illegitimate son, the weak Duke of Monmouth. The Duke of York was obviously the better choice, despite his Catholicism, and Charles had done what he could to bring the Duke of York back as a political power. When Parliament tried to exclude him from the succession, Charles dissolved it before it could act. When the anti-Catholic feeling lessened, Charles returned the Duke of York—and Pepys—to their former positions in the Admiralty.

With this problem seemingly resolved, Charles turned to his personal finances, and attempted to amass sufficient funds to provide for his more than a dozen illegitimate children. He also, strangely, started repaying old debts, including some contracted by his father. In 1684, he paid back 100 pounds that he had borrowed decades previously, when he had been Prince of Wales.

Charles's tight finances did not stop the dancing and feasting at Whitehall Palace. On Sunday, February 1, 1685, when he visited Charles there, John Evelyn found the entertainment as lavish as ever. But when Charles awoke the next morning in the royal bedchamber, he had a seizure. The royal physicians bled him and applied blisters and pans of coals to every part of his body, and when Charles failed to rouse, they forced emetics down his throat.

For several days Charles hung on, but it became apparent he was nearing his end. The Duke of York bent over his wan face and asked a question. "Yes, with all my heart," the King was heard to answer. The royal bedchamber was cleared of all but a faithful few, and a Catholic priest was smuggled in in disguise. The priest gave Charles the last rites and received him into the Catholic Church. Lingering a few more hours, Charles managed one last witticism—apologizing for taking so long to die. And then at dawn, he died.

The Duke of York, who ascended the throne as James II, tried to force his Catholicism on an unwilling nation.

CHARLES DIES

He issued a Declaration of Indulgence similar to Charles's which gave religious freedom to Catholics and nonconforming Protestants, and he ordered the clergy to read it from their pulpits.

The nation rebelled and made overtures to James's daughter Mary, who was married to William, Prince of Orange—a Protestant and the most prominent political leader in Holland. William and Mary were invited to come and rule England, and in 1689 they arrived, deposing James in an almost bloodless revolution.

Throughout these political changes, Wren kept rebuilding. By 1696—three decades after the fire—all fifty-one churches had been completed, except for a few remaining towers. Only St. Paul's was still unfinished. Month after month, year after year, work on the great cathedral continued. Wren was now in his sixties, but three times a week he let himself be hauled up by bucket to the top of the high cathedral so that he could make sure it was being constructed properly. The eight supports were set in place to hold up the dome. The forty-two columns in the colonnade were erected. In December, 1697, the choir was opened for divine services, and two years later, the morning chapel was completed.

By 1702, both William and Mary had died, and Queen Anne, another daughter of James II, came to the throne. By now Pepys had retired and, taking his books, had gone to live with Will Hewer, his former confidential secretary who had become wealthy. Then, the following year, at the age of seventy, Pepys died. John Evelyn made a solemn entry in his diary: "This day died Mr. Samuel Pepys, a very worthy, industrious, and curious person, none in England exceeding him in knowledge of the Navy."

The infirmities of old age prevented Evelyn from serving as a pallbearer for Pepys, who was "for near forty years so much my particular friend." Evelyn had continued to fill minor government and voluntary posts and had recently sublet Sayes Court to Peter the Great, the Russian Czar who had come to England to learn shipbuilding at Deptford. In 1706, Evelyn died, leaving Wren the only surviving link to the great fire.

On and on Wren worked, to complete St. Paul's. In 1710, when the dome was finished, a ceremony was held, and Wren, now almost eighty, watched from below as his son Christopher was raised to the top of the lantern in the cathedral's cupola, where he laid the highest stone.

Minor construction remained, and the aged Wren had to deal with clergy and government officials not even living when he had begun his monumental project. Several years previously he had had a dispute with some Parliament members over St. Paul's fence. Wren had used wrought iron; his critics claimed cast iron would have been "ten times mores durable." Before the controversy ended, Parliament invoked a little-known clause in the Act that had provided the legislation for rebuilding St. Paul's. It said that until the cathedral's construction was completed, the salary of its builder could be stopped. Wren had received only 13,000 pounds for rebuilding all London's churches, and his wages for rebuilding St. Paul's were only 200 pounds a year. To obtain his stopped pay, Wren petitioned everyone from Queen Anne to the House of Commons.

Shortly before she died in 1714, Queen Anne saw that Wren received all the monies he was owed. The Act of Settlement passed during her reign gave the succession to the nearest Protestant heir, who was Sophia, electress of

Hanover, the granddaughter of James I. Her son, George I, became the next King of England, and soon after his arrival from Germany, he appointed new commissioners to represent him in supervising the final stages of St. Paul's construction. The commissioners began imposing their ideas on Wren, and friction developed. In 1718, Wren, who for almost a half century had been the Surveyor General of His Majesty's Works, was summarily dismissed.

Once every year after, Wren came back to St. Paul's, where he would sit under the dome and look around, reflecting and thinking. After his visit in 1723, when he was ninety-one, he returned home and ate supper alone. Either that night or the following night—no one knows for sure—a servant found him dead in a dining-room chair. Wren was buried in the crypt of St. Paul's, the great cathedral he had rebuilt. The famous inscription in Latin over his burial place was composed by his son, and translated reads: Reader, if it is a monument you seek, look around you.

With Wren gone, evidence of the great fire began to disappear into history. Barely a decade after his death, the Fleet canal was bridged over, its warehouses turned into a road. The Thames quay lasted for a century, but became increasingly encroached on by sheds and warehouses. In the nineteenth century, the annual ceremony held in St. Paul's to commemorate the great fire was finally abandoned. The coal tax—which had paid for rebuilding of the city's public buildings, churches, and St. Paul's—continued to be collected long after the rebuilding had been completed, and not until the end of the nineteenth century was it appealed, mostly at the urging of Lord Randolph Churchill, Winston's father.

Today, one of the few reminders of the great fire of

London is the two-hundred-and-two-foot-high Monument. Designed by Wren and erected about one hundred feet west of Pudding Lane where the fire started, it was built in 1677 to "preserve the memory of this dreadful visitation." On the south side of the Monument words are inscribed that tell the story of the rebuilding dramatically if not accurately: "London rises again, whether with greater speed or magnificence is doubtful," it reads. "Three short years complete that which was considered the work of an age."

Hundreds had contributed to rebuilding the new London—Sir Christopher Wren above all—but looming over the city as its chief architect is the heroic image of Charles II. It was he who met with courage and perception a calamity that would have paralyzed most national leaders. It was he who cut through the plans of dreamers and provided the practical blueprint for rebuilding the city, restoring its trade, and rehousing its populace.

No one can visualize the Great Fire of London without seeing Charles knee-deep in mud, his royal finery dripping with water, passing buckets to fire fighters. Or Charles riding out to Moorfields and—with the City smoking behind him—assuring his homeless subjects that he, their King, would by the grace of God live and die with them. Or a few days later when, in his extraordinary proclamation, Charles set down the guidelines for the new London. And in the hectic months that followed when he worked day and night with City officials, his Privy Council, Parliament, and others to draw up the legislation that would make the rebuilding of London possible.

The morning Charles died in the royal bedchamber at

COLUMN COMMEMORATING THE GREAT FIRE

Whitehall Palace, he made a request of the faithful clus-
tered around his bed. "Open the curtains that I may once
more see day," he said. As light flooded in the windows, the
voices of workmen on the Thames could be heard, but
Charles could not see the new London he had inspired
and planned.

No longer was London a crowded city, cluttered with
hovels, slums, and jerry-built buildings. Now thousands of
neat red-brick homes—all built to specifications—lined
newly paved streets. London's houses now fronted streets
in regular lines, and for the first time since Roman days, a
Londoner could walk down a street without having to
change direction to avoid a pillar or house. No houses now

LONDON REBUILT

had second stories that projected over streets, blocking out light. No rainspouts sent water splashing in the faces of passersby; and garbage no longer ran down gutters in the middle of streets.

Streets now had sidewalks for pedestrians, and were wide enough to accommodate all carts and carriages that might come down them. Street corners had been widened, curves straightened, and grades leveled. Markets and water conduits no longer blocked main thoroughfares.

London had rid itself of the Plague. No longer would a child have to survive this terrible contagion in order to reach adulthood. London was now the "healthiest" city in the world, and because the "noisome trades" had all been relocated, its air was sweet and clean.

The city's nine thousand new houses of brick and stone, greatly lessened the chances of another sweeping fire. And London's modern fire defenses also protected the city as never before. Fireplugs installed along important streets, an improved system of fire watches, larger supplies of buckets, squirts, ladders and pickaxes in public buildings—these were only a few of the new fire-protection devices adopted. Londoners also for the first time had fire insurance.

As significant as the physical rebuilding of London were the advances made in its City government. Instead of a medieval organization in which municipal responsibilities were divided up among many wards and parishes, the city now had one central government which performed all municipal functions. Instead of constables in each ward being in charge of cleaning streets, there were now sewer commissioners whose responsibility covered the entire city. There were also street-paving commissioners, who had even the power to tax. Now Londoners could be proud of their city—not just of their parish or ward.

The Great Fire of London had destroyed the provincial capital of the Tudors and the Stuarts. In its place had arisen the most modern city in the world.

Bibliography

MORE THAN ONE hundred different sources—ranging from John Evelyn's diary to seventeenth-century illustrations of London before and after 1666—were consulted in writing this book on the Great Fire of London. However, principal sources were:

Bedford, John. *London's Burning*. New York: Abelard-Schuman, 1966.

Bell, Walter George. *The Great Fire of London in 1666*. London: John Lane, The Bodley Head, Ltd., 1920.

Bryant, Arthur. *Restoration England*. London: William Collins, Sons & Co. Ltd., 1960.

De Maré, Eric. *London's River*. New York: McGraw-Hill Book Company, 1965.

Hearsey, John E. N. *London and The Great Fire*. London: John Murray Publishers Ltd., 1965.

Henry, Robert. *London*. New York: E. P. Dutton & Co., Inc., 1949.

Pepys, Samuel. *Diary*. New York: Random House, Inc. (Modern Library edition).

Priestly, Harold. *London: The Years of Change*. London: Frederick Muller Ltd., 1966.

Rasmussen, Steen Eiler. *London: The Unique City*. Baltimore: Penguin Books, Inc., 1960.

Reddaway, T. F. *The Rebuilding of London after the Great Fire*. London: Jonathan Cape Ltd., 1940.

Wilson, John Harold. *The Private Life of Mr. Pepys*. New York: Farrar, Straus & Cudahy, Inc., 1959.

Index